GRADUATE STUDIES
TEXAS TECH UNIVERSITY

The Contemporary Peruvian Theatre

Robert J. Morris

No. 15

November 1977

Graduate Studies No. 15
98 pp.
18 November 1977
$6.00

Graduate Studies are numbered separately and published on an irregular basis under the auspices of the Dean of the Graduate School and Director of Academic Publications, and in cooperation with the International Center for Arid and Semi-Arid Land Studies. Copies may be obtained on an exchange basis from, or purchased through, the Exchange Librarian, Texas Tech University, Lubbock, Texas 79409.

Texas Tech Press, Lubbock, Texas

1977

CONTENTS

PREFACE

The purpose of this study is to examine the dramatic production of those writers who have made substantial contributions to the Peruvian theatre since the end of the Second World War. The need for a study of the type herein undertaken becomes obvious when one considers that there is no compendium of the recent developments in Peru's theatre and dramatic arts. In fact, it is surprising that the sources of information on this topic consist primarily of brief articles on the production of certain playwrights and, occasionally on individual works. Until now, there has existed no study that discusses the development of this theatre within an historical perspective and that includes the significant dramatists and their works within such a framework.

Some comments on Peru's contemporary theatre may be gleaned from Estuardo Núñez' *La literatura peruana en el siglo XX* (1965). However, it must be noted that these remarks are largely superficial and that the data are frequently incorrect. *La literatura peruana* (1965), by Augusto Tamayo Vargas, professor of Peruvian literature at the University of San Marcos, also mentions some aspects of recent developments in the dramatic arts in Peru, but in no way could this study be considered anything more than cursory. The principal criticism which must be leveled against Tamayo Vargas' work is that it is too general; it is briefer even than that of Núñez. Also, Peru's theatre has been largely ignored outside of that country, except for the treatment it received in Willis Knapp Jones' *Behind Spanish American Footlights* (1966). Although Jones devoted a chapter to the Peruvian drama, the greater portion of his presentation was dedicated to the years preceding 1946. It is apparent also that he did not always have accurate and sufficient data at his disposal because his evaluation of some authors is clearly questionable and, in many instances, suggests that he was not acquainted with a work well enough to judge its merits.

It is obvious that there is a need for a study that, in addition to being up to date, is not so brief as to depend on unsubstantiated generalities and that can afford its readers an overall understanding of the men and works that have most influenced the last twenty-five years of Peruvian drama. This study is primarily intended to fill that need and is addressed to all those who seek either a general introduction to this theatre or specific data on works which, in many instances, are difficult to obtain even in Peru.

The Introduction to this study provides, among other things, a brief background of the major trends in the Peruvian theatre from the first half of the nineteenth century to the end of the 1930's. In addition to this information, some emphasis has been placed on the important events that have had a noticeable effect in stimulating a renewal of interest in drama throughout Peru since the 1940's. These events include the founding of the nation's principal theatrical groups, their individual concerns as dramatic groups, and their separate contributions to the country's recent advancements in the dramatic arts. Also included in the Introduction is a discussion of the reasons for choosing 1946 as the year marking the beginning of Peru's dramatic renewal.

The basic corpus of this study follows the Introduction. Chapters 1, 2, and 3 are dedicated respectively to delineating the first years in the development of the new theatre, a discussion of writers and works that later appeared and continued the initial steps toward renewal, and observations on the most recent writers and works to reach the stage. At the beginning of the section on each writer, biographical information and a summation of the author's entire dramatic production are provided. The consideration of each play is introduced by a brief plot summary followed by an analysis of the most pertinent aspects of the work. Particular attention has been given to the use of language and various aspects of style, structural arrangement, characterization, and other elements that are useful in bringing to the fore the basic characteristics of the work and of the author's general dramatic tendencies. After the analysis of each writer's production, an overall evaluation of his dramatic production and his contributions to Peru's theatrical renewal is offered. In this respect it should be noted that the Peruvian theatre since 1946 is best described as a personal effort. As the results of this study indicate, there have been no national or predominant trends or schools that warrant thematic or subject matter groupings of either authors or works. Any such attempt would be artificial for the most part and would constitute a denial of the individuality that has characterized the Peruvian theatre since the end of the Second World War.

I would like to thank especially those who have been instrumental in uncovering many works that otherwise would have been unavailable: Dr. Ugarte Chamorro, Director of the Teatro de la Universidad de San Marcos; Jaime Saldías, Secretary of the drama group, Histrión, and Secretary of the Teatro de la Universidad de San Marcos; Ricardo Blume, a nationally known actor and past director of the Teatro de la Universidad Católica; and Ricardo Roca Rey, the past director of the Asociación de Artistas Aficionados. The cooperation of these aficionados of the Peruvian theatre has been of considerable value in this study. I am also indebted to the *Latin American Theatre Review* for permission to reproduce my studies on Salazar Bondy, Ortega, Ríos, and Alegría. Finally, I wish to acknowledge my gratitude to Russell H. Walker for his personal kindness and support that was indispensable to the realization of this work.

INTRODUCTION

During the past two decades there have been a number of significant developments in the Peruvian theatre. Some of them have been so impressive, in fact, that it seems feasible to refer to Peru's recent progress in the dramatic arts as outstanding. This dramatic awakening, or renewal, is particularly worthy of attention when viewed in the light of Peru's rather mediocre achievements during the past century.

Until the early years of national independence at the beginning of the nineteenth century, the theatre in Peru was for the most part a reflection of dramatic currents emanating from France and Spain. Indeed, a theatre of national design did not develop in Peru until the appearance of such dramatists as Felipe Pardo y Aliaga (1806-1868) and Manuel Asencio Segura (1805-1871). Even though Pardo y Aliaga's works were didactic and not as deeply rooted in Peruvian tradition as those of his renowned contemporary, he must be credited with the first successful drama with costumbrista elements in Peru—his *Frutos de la educación* premiered in Lima in 1830. It was followed by his two remaining masterpieces, *Huérfano en Chorrillos* (1833) and *Don Leocadio o el aniversario de Ayacucho* (1834), both of which emphasize the national customs of that period and have clearly defined regionalistic elements.

Although Pardo y Aliaga was the more refined dramatist stylistically, Segura was the more popular among his contemporaries due to the strong costumbrista appeal of his works and to his ability to dramatize the limeño way of life. Segura's initial piece was the one-act *Sargento Canuto* (1830), and as a result of the immediate triumph of this work, he was prompted to compose a number of others, several of which have become Peruvian classics: *La saya y manto* (1842), *La moza mala* (1855), and *Ña Catita* (1856). Segura was milder in criticizing his compatriots and their customs than was Pardo y Aliaga, and he dominated the Peruvian stage for thirty years. Other dramatists, encouraged by the inspirational success of Pardo y Aliaga and Segura, began to emphasize certain costumbrista and regionalistic elements in their own works. Nonetheless, the theatre in Peru began a slow decline after the death of Segura, and there was little deviation from the costumbrista trend until the late 1940's.

Not even the influence of Romanticism, which was evident as early as 1850 in Peru, was enough to restrain the enduring popularity of costumbrismo in the theatre, as well as in other literary forms. This was largely because the country did not produce any outstanding Romantic dramatists and because the theatre-going public at the time was generally unenthusiastic toward European-style Romanticism and particularly toward works devoid of national interests. In fact, only Benjamín Luis Cisnero, Ricardo Palma, and Nicolás Corpancho were even moderately successful as Romantic dramatists. Cisnero's two most important dramas were *El pabellón peruano* (n.d.) and *Alfredo el Sevillano* (n.d.), both of which are indicative of Cisnero's stylistic and thematic dependence on Spain's Romantic dramatist José Zorrilla. Ricardo Palma, best known for his inimitable brief narratives, the *Tradiciones peruanas*, also attracted some attention as a dramatist with such typically Romantic pieces as *La hermana del verdugo* (n.d.) and *La muerte o la libertad* (n.d.). In 1852, he wrote *Rodil*, but evidently he disliked the play and never allowed its premiere. Exactly one century later, it was discovered by José Jiménez Borja in a Lima library and published in a Peruvian literary journal, *Mar del Sur*. In 1852, Nicolás Corpancho wrote *El poeta cruzado*, which is considered among the best of Peru's Romantic dramas. Yet it and *El templario* (1855), a continuation of his former work, is an unmistakable reflection of the Spanish Romantic influence. Corpancho's third drama, *El Barquero y el Virrey*, which premiered after his death, was not as successful as the two previous plays and was never given a second run. Such was the fate of almost all of Peru's Romantic dramas since, with practically no exceptions and despite the fact that they were often close imitations of the Spanish Romantic masterpieces, they were characteristically superficial and, despite their regionalistic elements, failed to sustain public interest.

The beginning of the twentieth century brought little appreciable change in the Peruvian theatre. Most of the works produced until the late 1930's were largely a commercialized continuation of the Romantic and costumbrista theatre of the 1800's. The most prominent dramatists of these four decades include Ladislao F. Meza (1892-1925), who is often referred to as Peru's last Romantic; José Chioino (1898); and Leonidas Yerovi (1881-1917). Ladislao Meza, who is similar to the famous Uruguayan dramatist Florencio Sánchez in some respects as a result of his preoccupation with social injustices, is best remembered for his naturalistic works set in the slums of Lima: *Ciudad misteriosa*, *El tablado de los miserables*, *La miseria del triunfador*, and *La isla de los perros*. José Chioino's first work, *Retorno*, appeared in 1928. Since that time, he has been the costumbrista dramatist par excellence of the whole of Peru. His most successful plays include *La divina canción* (1923), *Una vez en la vida* (1927), *Novio de emergencia* (1928), and *La propia comedia* (1947). Chioino's last work, *Tabú* (1950), was awarded the 1950 drama prize given by the Municipality of Lima. Because he has had such an extended career and has made undeniable contributions to the contemporary theatre in Peru, additional observations on his importance are offered in the following chapter. Leonidas Yerovi was one of Peru's most versatile playwrights during the early twentieth century. His series of box office successes began with *La de cuatro mil* in 1903, and continued with *Tarjetas postales* (1905), *Salsa roja* (1913), and *La gente loca* (1914). Yerovi had just reached the peak of his career when he was assassinated in 1917, and there is little doubt about the subsequent influence that his death had on the creeping deterioration and lethargy in Peru's drama. The decline had begun with the waning of Romanticism about 1900, and by 1920 Peru's theatrical activities were practically at a standstill, inasmuch as only a few works, largely unsuccessful, were written. In addition to the paucity of works, there were too few professional or amateur groups in Peru to present the works that were available.

Before proceeding to the discussion of those events, works, and individuals which are particularly kindred to the truly contemporary theatre in Peru, it seems appropriate to note that works of indigenous orientation have been a perennial favorite of Peruvian audiences during the past one hundred years. As a unique regionalistic, if not nationalistic expression, this drama usually takes its inspiration from some aspect of Indian tradition or legend, and is clearly designed to laud the ancient heritage of the modern Peruvian. The most famous of these works, *Ollantay*, was supposedly written by Antonio Valdés during the eighteenth century. Since the mid-nineteenth century there has been a multitude of adaptations with titles the same as the original, such as those by Pacheco Zegarro in 1887, Constantino Carrasco in 1878, Ricardo Rojas (Argentina) in 1939, and Salazar Bondy and César Miró in 1953. Indigenous drama of original composition was also popular in the first half of the twentieth century, as evidenced by these recent contributions: *Pacha Huayta* (1947) by Pedro Macassi, *Sueño en los Andes* (1947) by Oscar Silva, and the works of Andrés Alencastre, published in 1950 as *Dramas y comedias del Ande*. Despite their popularity, particularly with the rural population, the influence of these indigenous works, as well as that of the costumbrista and Romantic drama, has had little if any impact on Peru's dramatic development since 1946, and it is worthy of note that a number of these works have never been presented in Lima.

With the beginning of the second World War and the end of the second Spanish Republic, Peru, as well as the rest of Hispanic America, entered into a new period of economic affluence and increased public awareness of international affairs. One of the important consequences of these economic and sociological phenomena was that many of the South American countries began to undergo an awakening of their literary consciousness, which was to affect the entire national perspective, including that of the theatre. In Peru, for example, the concerned cosmopolitan began to increase his efforts to attain a level of cultural achievement equal to that of his peers in the more advanced nations, and, ultimately, took important steps towards improving such entertainment media as the theatre.

Shortly, and despite the abject situation of its national theatre, a renewal of interest in the drama was born among artists and intellectuals who saw in the theatre a suitable vehicle for providing, among other things, a wider and more significant view of the nation and the world. The number of playwrights increased and many of them were quick to focus their attention on Peruvian as well as international problems. As a result, their works began to expose the profound universal changes that were taking place and, as their area of interest expanded, the Peruvian theatre soon moved toward the abandonment of the regionalistic and costumbrista formulas of the preceding generations to offer a more intuitive and poetic interpretation of reality, contemporary themes, and man in general.

The most obvious indication of Peru's desire to escape its traditional theatrical past was the appearance of three award-winning poetic dramas in the 1946-1947 period: *Esa luna que empieza* (1946) by Percy Gibson Parra, *Don Quijote*

(1946) by Juan Ríos, and *Amor, Gran laberinto* (1947) by Sebastián Salazar Bondy. These works were the first to suggest that there was a definite concern with the dilemma of Peru's tradition-oriented drama, and they were promptly recognized by most literary historians and critics as the most significant plays written in Peru since the beginning of the twentieth century. These same works mark the historical beginning of the renaissance of the contemporary Peruvian theatre. When viewed collectively, they, more than the authors themselves, are responsible for the spirit of renewal that has continued to characterize every aspect of the theatre arts in Peru.

As interest grew in renewing Peru's prominence among the nations of South America that took pride in their drama, a number of encouraging incentives were offered to the many new writers who were beginning to compose their own dramatic works. One such encouragement was the founding and development of new and energetic theatrical groups, such as the Asociación de Artistas Aficionados (which debuted in 1938) and the Teatro de la Universidad de San Marcos (in 1941). Among the most impressive of the new groups was the Compañía Nacional de Comedias, founded in 1945 and totally supported by the federal government. Although such evidence of moral and financial encouragement by the government was the most important incentive to that time, it was not until the following year, 1946, that the national parliament made what has become one of the most enduring contributions to the renewal of the national theatre by establishing and providing funds for the annual Premio Nacional de Teatro. Even though the award is not the country's most economically rewarding—it is only 10,000 soles—it has since become Peru's most coveted and prestigious drama award.

The formation of the Escuela Nacional de Arte Escénico (E.N.A.E.) in 1946 also contributed in no small way to Peru's drama renewal. Until 1948, when it was replaced by the Instituto de Arte Dramático, the E.N.A.E. was the most active theatrical group in Peru. Composed of experienced actors, directors, and technicians, the E.N.A.E. served as an instructional organization and sponsored annual classes in the dramatic arts, was a valuable incentive for the increasing number of playwrights (annually financing the printing of a number of modern Peruvian plays), produced many award-winning plays for the first time, and generally played a unique role in the country's theatrical advancements. By the time of the awarding of the first Premio Nacional de Teatro in 1946, aficionados and playwrights were well aware of the activities of such independent groups as the E.N.A.E. and their role in helping the country break away from its stagnant dramatic past.

The new Peruvian theatre steadily improved between 1947 and 1948 as suggested by the increased number of works characterized by marked universal, psychological, and poetic tendencies. By 1950, the dramatic renewal in Peru no longer seemed to be a remote possibility due to the obvious severance of many of the bonds of tradition and to the constant effort to find new and more adequate means of dramatic expression. Less than five years after the first Premio Nacional de Teatro was given, the Peruvian theatre had made several important advancements: it was on an elevated poetic level in its conception and expression of human values; it was markedly varied in its themes and subject matter; it was becoming a theatre full of suggestions and symbols; and the monologue and relatively short pieces were becoming increasingly popular.

The number of dramatic pieces written during the mid-1950's was surprising, yet only a few of these works were ever presented. Nonetheless, the critics and aficionados were undaunted, because they tended to base their bright outlook for the country's theatrical future on the quantity rather than on the overall quality of the works. They also defended their predictions for a promising future, maintaining that the theatre still suffered from a lack of skilled technicians and trained personnel. Fortunatley, public and private zeal did not wane and the seriousness of the problem of presentation diminished as several new theatrical groups were formed: Teatro de la Universidad Católica (1951), Club de Teatro (1953), and Histrión (1956). It is also worthy of note that interest in the foreign theatre increased during the mid-1950's due to the numerous dramatic groups which were visiting the country or being established by resident nonnationals.

Peru's efforts to improve its theatre during 1957 and 1958 were even more productive than before. A new generation of young writers was beginning to express itself successfully and without serious opposition from older writers. The problem of quantity over quality still remained, but there was also a definite increase in the percentage of excellent plays presented within the national boundaries. The most important and acclaimed dramatic achievement of the decade came in 1959 when Solari Swayne's *Collacocha* premiered in Lima. It is of interest that this play was written in Peru in 1955 and was applauded in Mexico and Colombia in 1958 and 1959 before its triumphant presentation in Lima. But since its initial presentation in Mexico, it has been internationally recognized as the outstanding drama written by a Peruvian in this century.

The number of publishing dramatists and active theatrical groups in Peru increased during the 1960's, but only a few works, such as *Los desesperados* by Juan Ríos, *El Rabdomante* by Sebastián Salazar Bondy, and *Vida y pasión de Santiago el pajarero* by Julio Ramón Ribeyro, met with more than moderate acclaim. This does not mean, however, that Peru's dramatic renewal is at a standstill. Since the mid-1960's, for instance, the more established theatre groups have had to compete with newer groups, and several young playwrights such as Alonso Alegría, Julio Ortega, Sara Joffré and Victor Zavala have appeared to affirm their continuing support of the national theatre renewal. The most important consideration, however, is that this latest generation of groups and playwrights has been unusually successful in promoting a theatre that, for the first time in Peru, is primarily experimental in spirit and poetic and universal in design.

A second indication of the favorable dramatic climate since the 1960's is that public interest in the theatre is at this century's peak. In fact, during recent years several theatrical groups have had to extend their run of a play of national or foreign origin in order to satisfy public demand. The most recent incentive and indication of the expanding support for the national theatre was the establishment, in 1966, of the Premio Nacional for works in one act and for monologues. These annual contests are sponsored by the Dirección Nacional de Teatro, which guarantees that the first place works will be printed and distributed gratuitously and will be presented by the Teatro de la Universidad de San Marcos within one year of the award.

The Teatro de la Universidad de San Marcos is one of the few groups in Lima to have its own locale. Some other groups, such as the Asociación de Artistas Aficionados, Teatro de la Universidad Católica, and Histrión, also enjoy their own facilities; nonetheless, the competition among these and other groups to secure a larger or preferred site for producing a play is often keen. Lima's only large theatres are the Teatro Municipal and the Teatro Segura, and these are frequently in demand for events other than the staging of dramatic works.

As one might expect, the surging renewal of interest in the theatre has resulted in the formation of numerous theatrical groups since 1950. While many of these have been shortlived, there are several which have become relatively successful as attested by their number of productions, the size and experience of their casts, and their fairly stable economic situations. Since the 1950's, four groups have come to the fore as the most influential and accomplished in the Capital City. The oldest of these, formed in 1938, is the Asociación de Artistas Aficionados (A.A.A.), which, since its founding, has particularly allied itself with the modern theatre in Peru. This group is supported by a large cast of experienced actors, and has regularly employed two of Peru's most respected directors, Luis Álvarez and Ricardo Roca Rey. While the A.A.A.'s dramatic interests and repertoire are wide in scope, it also regularly presents the national favorites of past and contemporary origin.

The Club de Teatro was established in 1953 as a result of the inspiration of Sebastián Salazar Bondy and the direction of Reynaldo D'Amore. This group was an outgrowth of Salazar Bondy's early concern with the lack of both modern trends in Peru's theatre and of groups sufficiently oriented toward contemporary dramatic expression. As a result, the repertoire of the Club de Teatro consists principally of foreign works, since there has been a consistent lack of national drama offering contemporary themes and technical advancements. The Club de Teatro, even from its beginning, has been a small company, and the size of its audience is always limited by the restricted seating capacity of Negro-Negro, a night club leased by the group.

Histrión was founded in late 1956 and made its debut in 1957. Since then it has been one of Lima's most active groups. Its cast is composed largely of amateurs whose esprit de corps is undoubtedly their greatest strength. Many of Peru's most accomplished playwrights have been attracted to Histrión by the group's serious dedication to the dramatic arts and by the assurance of finding there other devotees of diverse interests and talents. Histrión has not only offered invaluable opportunities to actors and technicians of limited experience, but, also, its attempt to motivate public awareness of national authors is evident in the fact that almost half of its repertoire is of Peruvian authorship.

The last of these four groups is the Teatro de la Universidad de San Marcos (T.U.S.M.) which was founded in 1941 and was quite active until the 1950's when it faltered and entered a period of lethargy. Then, in 1960 it underwent a total reorganization and once again became one of the nation's outstanding theatrical groups. Since then, the group's repertoire, which has always been oriented toward foreign works, has been considerably enhanced by the inclusion of many plays of national origin. T.U.S.M. is also the only one of these four groups that can be described as truly nonprofessional and nonprofit, for its cast and technicians are university students who work under the guidance of Dr. Guillermo Ugarte Chamorro. T.U.S.M. also houses the Centro de Investigaciones de Teatro Peruano, which, in collaboration with the theatre group, sponsors free summer courses for drama study, numerous formal discussions and lectures on the theatre, and the publication of a number of plays and research papers, as well as determining the winning works in the national contest for one-act drama and monologues.

Among the remaining groups in Lima, there are two which are especially active, and, if their past performances are any indication of their future achievements, they are destined to become mainstays. The first is the Teatro de la Universidad Católica (T.U.C.), which, founded in 1961, had presented more than forty works by the end of 1974. At the present, T.U.C.'s locale has a small seating capacity, several adjoining classrooms, and a rapidly growing library with mimeograph facilities. The T.U.C. is similar to T.U.S.M. in that it, too, is concerned with all aspects of the dramatic arts from actual productions to intellectual debates. The Instituto Nacional de Arte Dramático, which replaced the Escuela Nacional de Arte Escénico in 1958, is totally financed by the national government, and offers a five-year course of study leading to degrees in Dramatic Arts. This group's repertoire is somewhat limited in comparison with those of such groups as Histrión, but is has been responsible for some of the recent stage successes in Lima.

There are, of course, other theatrical groups in Lima, but they are not so professionally oriented as those already mentioned, and, because of their recent founding, most have a limited repertoire. Among the most promising of these groups are the Compañía Lucía Irurita, Nuevo Teatro Ofelia Woloshin, El Carroussell, and El Teatro Nacional Popular. The latter group, which was founded in 1971 and is under the direction of Alonso Alegría, is federally financed and is intended to propagandize the political dictates of the government at the grassroots level. Unfortunately, the group has yet to establish any kind of reputation since it has presented few plays and has met with some budgetary difficulties.

Thus it is that the post-World War II theatre in Peru was given new hope with the concurrence of established, though struggling, theatre groups and the appearance of outstanding works by national dramatists. Together, they quickly found approval and support with their public and, as a result, flourished in a way few national theatres have in this century. As the following chapters will show, during the past three decades, the Peruvian theatre has been characterized by a sustained search for excellence and a constant renewal of its standards and goals.

RENAISSANCE OF THE NEW THEATRE

As one reviews the development of the Peruvian theatre during the past century, it is apparent that no period has been more significant historically or indicative of future change than the fourteen months between August 1946 and October 1947. During this time three works by as many playwrights were presented and marked the new route the national theatre was to take in order to sever its bonds of tradition and liberate itself from a stagnant past. These works constitute Peru's entry into a theatre of contemporary design and appeal and, ultimately, of universal awareness. It is of note that, of these three dramatists, Sebastián Salazar Bondy and Juan Ríos continued to write and, together, dominated the national theatre until their productions ceased. The third playwright, Percy Gibson Parra, wrote only one play, yet its appearance at such a crucial moment of the theatre, coupled with its undeniable artistic merits and its implied renovation of the national dramatic norms, have guaranteed his prominence in the annals of Peruvian literature.

Gibson was born in Arequipa in 1908 and from 1929 to 1934 lived in Spain and traveled in other European countries. Since 1947 he has been the Secretary General of the National Library in Lima. While he has produced some poetry and essays, his reputation as a writer rests on *Esa luna que empieza*, which shared the first Premio Nacional de Teatro in 1946 with *Don Quijote* by Juan Ríos.[1] Gibson's play is a three-act "poema escénico" structured on the daily life of several inhabitants of a simple fishing village. Yet the appeal and success of the work does not hinge on any regionalistic focus. *Esa luna que empieza* is, instead, a lyric dramatization of the universal and eternal themes of birth, love and death. Gibson's symbol of the eternal flux, of life itself, is the story of the personal tragedy and triumph of the characters. In a manner reminiscent of the symbolist Maeterlinck, Gibson's is a simple drama with no intrigue or circumstancial conflicts to obscure his esthetic observance of man's transcendental significance. For some, there is also the apparent influence of the poet-dramatist Lorca as such natural and symbolic phenomena as the waning and waxing of the moon or the flow and ebb of the tide appear in symphony with the birth-death motif. Perhaps the most intriguing aspect of this work is that its success did not encourage its author to persevere as a dramatist. For many, this is the real tragedy of *Esa luna que empieza.*

Fortunately, there were other dramatists at the time, such as Juan Ríos, who also possessed the kind of talent and creative ambitions which Gibson was never to express again. In fact, Ríos,[2] the author of eight major plays between

1. Percy Gibson Parra, *Esa luna que empieza*, pp. 191-254, in *Teatro peruano contemporáneo*, ed. Aurelia Miró Quesada (Lima: Editorial Huascarán, 1948).

2. Juan Ríos Rey was born in Lima on 28 September 1941 and received his formal education in that capital. When the Spanish Civil War broke out in 1936, he fought with the Republican forces in the Sierra Guadarrama. He returned to Peru only to be exiled by the government of Marshall Oscar Benavides. After several years in Madrid as a correspondent, Ríos was afforded safe conduct in Peru with the establishment of the dictatorship of General Manuel A. Odría. Ríos organized the First National Convention of Writers and Artists in Lima, and during its convocation read and forged a controversial motion to outlaw the re-

1946 and 1960, was the only dramatist of his time to succeed with dramas free of national sociopolitical influences. The vitally stimulating role that Ríos has played in the renewal of the contemporary theatre in Peru has been accentuated by his winning the Premio Nacional de Teatro five times in fifteen years. He has won the award for *Don Quijote* (1946), *La selva* (1950), *Ayar Manko* (1952), *El mar* (1954), and *Los desesperados* (1960).

Despite his national acclaim, however, Ríos has been unduly overlooked by foreign critics and theatrical companies.[3] This ironic development is due partially to the fact that only two of his works, *Ayar Manko* and his first version of *Don Quijote*, were published before 1961. In that year appeared the only volume of his drama, containing *Don Quijote, El fuego, El reino sobre las tumbas, Los bufones, La selva,* and *Los desesperados. El mar,* his only other work known to exist, does not appear in this volume. Nonetheless, a manuscript has been secured, and a discussion of the drama is included in the following chronological listing of Ríos' dramas.

Don Quijote,[4] Ríos' first drama, was presented in 1946 and revised in 1957. As was previously mentioned, it was co-winner of the first Premio Nacional de Teatro in 1946. It is written in blank verse, usually in lines of more than sixteen syllables, and is divided into six cuadros. The first five cuadros are inspired by random episodes in the original novel and recall the knight's chivalresque folly as he pursues his dream. It is in the final segment that Ríos invests the drama with his originality. Don Quijote, now on his death bed, refuses to give up his dream, even though he is aware now of the mad adventures it has brought him. As he tells Sancho, it is man's dream that distinguishes him from the rock, which is inert and contributes nothing to life. Sancho finally understands his master and hands him his lance, the symbol of the knight's dream. Don Quijote is thus prepared to die, convinced that while his body will return to dust, his dream will live eternally. His last words reiterate Ríos' purpose for writing this play: "¡De mi cadáver puede crecer un mundo! ¡La muerte es bella/La muerte es pura! ¡La muerte es Vida!" (Ríos, *Teatro*, p. 136). They indicate that for Don Quijote, as for all men, it is man's dream that is immortal, and death as the absolute end of being does not exist.

Despite the popularity and favorable criticism that *Don Quijote* has received, the work is not sound dramatically. Its principal weakness is an excessive rhetorical dependence on the novel. In addition, this play, as do several of Ríos' dramas, includes frequent poetic interludes that detract from the play's aesthetic and thematic unity. The major interludes in it are clearly marked, however,

pressive laws of the dictatorship. For the past several years he has been a literary critic for a daily newspaper in Lima.

Ríos is also an important poet. In 1941, he published *Canción de siempre*, a collection of verse which evidences his early interest in classical literature. In 1948, he won the Premio Nacional de Poesía for *Cinco cantos a la agonía*, and in 1953 he repeated this triumph with *Cinco cantos al destino del hombre*.

3. At least two of Peru's most influential critics point to Ríos as one of the three major dramatists of post-World War II Peru. Augusto Tamayo Vargas, in his *Literatura peruana* and Estuardo Núñez, in his *La literatura peruana en el siglo XX*, unfortunately devote less than two pages apiece to Ríos' theatre.

4. Juan Ríos, *Don Quixote*, pp. 11-137, in *Teatro* by Ríos (Lima: n.p., 1961). Subsequent reference to this volume in text will be parenthetically indicated by Ríos, *Teatro*, and respective page numbers.

so that they can be omitted without detriment to the overall dramatic effect of the work. A third weakness is that Ríos' creative talents are often overshadowed by his allusion to too many episodes and by the inclusion of too many personages from the original novel.

With regard to the structural basis, the division into six cuadros clearly reinforces the episodic nature of the drama. Any division into longer segments would weaken the progression of the play action, and any division into shorter segments would invite chaos and jeopardize the dream defense in the final scene. It is apparent that Ríos took care to balance and proportion these segments so that the story development in the first five cuadros would parallel the original and so that the sixth would highlight his thematic presentation.

Don Quijote contains many of the dramatic elements and themes which appear in Ríos' subsequent production. One noticeable absence is that of an American setting and atmosphere. Yet, *Don Quijote* does contain the central motif of Ríos' total production: man's epic struggle for immortality. The basic irony in his theatre is that the story of man's struggle is usually accompanied by the dust-to-dust theme, or that of the inevitable return to nothingness. In all of his plays written after *Don Quijote*, Ríos' protagonists are ambitious and their deeds are motivated by a hate that results in their death. Thus, his works customarily portray an individual who suffers due to his own actions. The only escape from his world of death is death, often by suicide.

Don Quijote, therefore, cannot be considered a representative introduction to Ríos' subsequent creations. This is not to decry its merits. Foremost among these are its structural arrangement, its appeal to a universal Hispanic audience, and Ríos' imaginative portrayal of Don Quijote's refusal to give up his dream in the final moments of life.

El fuego,[5] which is written in blank verse and is divided into seven cuadros, is Ríos' first drama of American design. In this case he has adapted a classical myth to the Hispano-American scene and has wrapped the entire production in an epic mantle. *El fuego* is inspired by Aeschylus' classical version of the myth of Prometheus, who is honored as the founder of civilization.

The drama is set in an Andean republic during the early days of its independence. It tells of a rebel captain and his compatriots who battle to overthrow a national military junta that threatens to establish a dictatorship. The leader's most trusted companion in the campaign is the Fugitive, a merciless figure who constantly harangues the rebels with his passionate hatred of the enemy. He contends that economic class differences are the cause of national unrest, and that hate is the most powerful stimulant for motivating the underdog to abolish social inequality. The Captain agrees with the economic class barriers, but maintains that social correction should be served by justice tempered by compassion, not hate. By the sixth cuadro the enemy has surrounded the rebels, yet the Captain refuses an offer of amnesty because he is determined to win his symbolic battle. Although the rebel losses are heavy, he is undaunted

5. Ríos, *El fuego*, pp. 143-281, in *Teatro* by Ríos.

and feels self-sacrifice is the only way his dream of autonomy can be fulfilled. It is evident that martyrdom is the Captain's goal when he refuses to escape with the Fugitive.

The final scene dwells on the change that takes place in the Captain. He has been wounded in the side and chained to a rock in a manner reminiscent of the hero in *Prometheus Bound.* At this point, however, the Captain's Promethean qualities, his compassion and idealism, turn to bitter hatred for the enemy as he witnesses the execution of his followers. The Captain's new-found agony and his execution prompt a blind prophet to end the drama with the prediction that the Captain's dream will be nurtured in the hearts of others willing to shed blood for freedom and justice. The Captain, then, did not die in vain.

The inspirational indebtedness of *El fuego* to the myth of Prometheus should be evident to most audiences. Anyone familiar with the poetic heritage of Peru would also note the obvious influence of César Vallejo on Ríos' verse. In every cuadro, except the third and the fifth, the Captain recalls Vallejo's stoic resignation before the agony of his own existence. For example, in the first cuadro he reflects: "Ah, fatalidad, Tierra, Destino, ¡aparta de mi este caliz!" (Ríos, *Teatro*, p. 174). In the sixth he is anguished to think: " ¡Ahora bebo las heces de mi cáliz, / el fondo de lágrimas del indescriptible vino! / Ahora sé todo el sufrimiento que puede anidar en el pecho del hombre" (Ríos, *Teatro*, p. 260).[6] Despite Vallejo's influence, however, *El fuego* is victim of its author's poetic stagnation. Ríos simply fails to incorporate into his dialogues the poetic splendor for which he seems to strive. They are too flat, overly long, and repetitious. The unfortunate conclusion is that Ríos fails in his attempt to adapt the epic and heroic subject matter of his dream to original lyric prose.

El fuego is an episodic work much the same as *Don Quijote*, and, in the main, the division into seven cuadros is structurally sound. But the thematic significance of at least one cuadro, the fifth, is questionable and certainly weak. This segment, which is obviously included for its dramatic tension, depicts how the Fugitive's aplomb temporarily saves the Captain from death.

Despite the distinctions made between the major characters, *El fuego* is not a drama of psychological intent. Both of the characters are rather flat because, on a superior level of interpretation, they respectively represent man's instinctive bestiality and his emotional compassion. The Fugitive capitalizes on man's bestial instincts to forward his own beliefs throughout the drama. He ably arouses man's hate and will to kill. The Captain, on the other hand, has distinct difficulties in shaping an emotional compassion in his men. His plans and achievements are constantly thwarted by the Fugitive's efforts to instill hate in every follower. Due to the characters being stereotyped, therefore, the theme of the drama is not expressed, or evidenced, until the final scene when the Captain, too, condemns compassionate justice to herald force and hatred.

6. No single volume of Vallejo's poems seems to influence Ríos more than any other; however, *España, aparta de mí este cáliz* is certainly suggested by these lines from the drama. César Vallejo, *Poemas humanos. España, aparta de mí este cáliz* (Buenos Aires: Editorial Losada, 1961).

He dies a martyr, but the change in him remains a negative judgment of non-violent measures in the struggle for national autonomy.

It is hard to see *El fuego* as a valid indication of Ríos' dramatic capability, but it is important because it contains many of the major tendencies and themes that later are refined and become characteristic of his production. *El fuego*, for instance, seems to have been the inspiration for Ríos' *Los desesperados* (1960). It, too, evidences Ríos' growing desire to forge a truly Hispano-American theatre.

El reino sobre las tumbas[7] is a brief work in comparison with Ríos' other dramas. Written early in his career (1949), it is in blank verse and divided into two cuadros. Ríos' source of inspiration for the play is the classical story of the Forest of Nemi and, specifically, James Frazer's rendition of the myth of Diana of Aricia and Virbius, a god of the wood and chase who was worshipped with her. Virbius supposedly originated the custom of giving the priest's office to a runaway slave who, with a tree branch, killed the incumbent and assumed his position.[8]

With only minor innovations in the first cuadro, *El reino sobre las tumbas* is a faithful and artistically impressive adaptation of the myth. Ríos' original contribution is the story of Marcos, an outlaw who enters the forest to escape Roman soldiers. He does so aware that no man has ever left the forest, a kingdon of death ruled by Crotón, Marcos' long lost brother. The second cuadro has little to offer those familiar with the myth of Frazer's account. It dramatizes Crotón's escape from his agonizing solitude through death at the hands of his brother. By his act, Marcos has sealed his fate. Under the law of Diana, he has forsaken his liberty in order to defend the silent kingdom of the dead.

El reino sobre las tumbas is the most forceful expression of Ríos' dramatic themes and, in this regard, is his most succinct portrayal of an individual who rules over a kingdom of death and whose agonized existence is relieved only when life is terminated. In addition, this work is a marked improvement with regard to Ríos' frequent confusion of thematic currents resulting from the use of extraneous dramatic and tension-building episodes. In fact, this is one of the author's better productions because it is not a cluttered arrangement of his favorite themes. Nevertheless, the drama is not a model of Ríos' stylistic capabilities because it suffers from poetic verbosity. This does not mean that there is excessive rhetorical repetition or that its philosophic implications are poorly made. The point is that the main characters' dialogues are needlessly long and involved in several instances. Sometimes they suggest that the author is enjoying poetic exercise and license, having foregone the original intent of his writing.

Los bufones[9] was written in 1949 and, unlike many of Ríos' dramas, was never revised. This is a one-act work that takes place during the reign of Spain's

7. Ríos, *El reino sobre las tumbas*, pp. 287-328, in *Teatro* by Ríos.

8. Oskar Seyffert, *Dictionary of Classical Antiquities*, rev. and ed. Henry Nettleship and James E. Sandys (New York: Meridian, 1958), *s.v.* "Diana."

9. Ríos, *Los bufones*, pp. 333-378, in *Teatro* by Ríos.

Philip IV. The time is 1644, one year after the Spanish defeat at Rocroi. It is also the time when Philip's administrative duties have heavily increased and his wife is dying of a mysterious malady. The play dramatizes the efforts of one of Philip's buffoons to alleviate the King's agony.

Shortly after the curtain rises, Philip dejectedly enters and the buffoons commence their antics intended to amuse him. They fail to distract Philip because his worldly problems have led to a more profound and personal preoccupation. He is suffering the agony of being only mortal, and his obsessive concern with corporeal mortality has essentially isolated him from society.

Sebastián de Morra is an embittered buffoon who also suffers the agony of personal solitude. His hatred for the world stems from his feeling of social inferiority and his desire to be considered more than a simple buffoon. Despite the vast social differences between him and the King, however, Sebastián understands the cause of Philip's concern. And although he can proffer no lasting solace, Sebastián does remind Philip that each man is a mortal being for whom death is inevitable. He feels that life and its agonies are the figment of another's dream. When the dream is ended, man ceases to exist.

Sebastián also believes that the Queen is dying from the agony of solitude and that only he understands the real cause of her certain death. Thus, he is ironically elated to hear that her last words were for him. It is his proof that she accepted and confided in him as an equal human being. Sebastián no longer feels he is a simple buffoon, and his hate and pessimism are now dissipated. Philip's agony is also terminated by the death of his queen and by Sebastián's peculiar insight into his problem. The King now realizes the futility of yearning for corporeal immortality.

This work should be of special interest to anyone acquainted with *Los bufones*, a canvas by Velázquez. Such a nonliterary motivation is refreshing and points to Ríos' broad cultural background and inspiration. The manner in which the author has blended the Spanish inspiration with historical fact and his fictional portrayal of the King is particularly praiseworthy. *Los bufones* also is appealing because there is a natural flow of ideological currents throughout the drama. There are no digressions or even any displacement of the three traditional unities. It is the personal note which predominates, nonetheless, and the characterization of Philip and Sebastián are outstanding for their spontaneity and for being more natural than artificial or dramatic. For example, the familiar relations which exist between the King and his buffoon are startling at first, but as the games and antics continue, an intimate and congenial rapport is established between the actors and the audience. By the time the games have ended, Sebastián's words and actions do not seem out of place with regard to his social station, and Philip seems an ordinary human being. As a result, the final solution to the King's personal conflict is credible and free of any immediate psychological objections the audience may have had at the beginning of the drama.

The basic themes in this work are those found in most of Ríos' drama: hate, the agony of existence, inevitable death as the only escape, and social inequalities. And, as the friendship between the buffoon and the King is elaborated by the author, these themes are slowly introduced and developed by Sebastián—from the opening moments, in which his hate is manifested, to the closing moments, in which he feels accepted as a man equal to any other. In reality, therefore, the buffoon, and not the King, is responsible for originating the thematic currents of the drama.

Los bufones is written in blank verse, with lines of sixteen or more syllables predominating. This drama, unlike many others by Ríos, does not subject the audience to any unduly long or repetitious poetic passages. Its brevity and Ríos' apparent concern for preserving a natural fluidity complement each other so that there is no noticeable lapse in the dialogue.

Perhaps the most rewarding feature of the play is found in the development of the principal characters' interrelationship. This is true even though the bonds that unite Philip and Sebastián are cleverly hidden until the last moments of the play. In the closing scene there is a sober and significant realization that both characters have profited in a positive manner from Sebastián's hatred and agonized isolation from society. The use of hate as a major motivating factor is usually found in at least one character in each of Ríos' plays. In *Los bufones*, hatred is not championed as a future norm, as in *El fuego*, but is ironically influential in determining the characters' optimistic outlook on life.

Ríos' next drama, *La selva*,[10] was written in 1950 and won the Premio Nacional de Teatro the same year. It was revised slightly in 1960. The final version is in blank verse and is in three acts, with the last divided into two cuadros. The classical inspiration for this drama is clearly the story of Jason and the Argonauts. Ríos has adapted Jason's original adventures and love for Medea to a drama of the Spanish Conquest of the New World. He deviates slightly from the original, but not sufficiently to disguise the classical influence.

The basic story concerns a Spanish Captain who is sent to make conquests for the Crown but, failing that, falls in love with the daughter of his Indian captor. To prove her love and to effect the soldiers' escape, the Princess kills a brother and betrays her father. Once in civilization, she murders again to protect the Captain and, when faced with a vengeful mob, kills herself and her children to avoid further agony. She so dominates the Captain that he, too, joins her with his own suicide.

The drama actually begins eight years after the return to civilization. So, in order to dramatize past events, Ríos resorts to the use of flashbacks to maintain and relate the two levels of action, that of the past and of the present. These chronologically arranged interludes are introduced by the songs of the dreamer, or soñador, and occur throughout the work inasmuch as almost one-half of it takes place in the past. It should be noted that the use of flashbacks in the drama represents a skillful complement to Ríos' departure from the traditional linear plot development. Their distribution and timing facilitate the relation of past events to respective present time action. The potential time prob-

10. Ríos, *La selva*, pp. 383-524, in *Teatro* by Ríos.

lem in this drama is deftly solved by Ríos' handling of the flashbacks. They are an unexpected addition to, yet his only deviation from, his traditionally oriented dramaturgy.

Among Ríos' drama heretofore discussed, *La selva* is the most complex and artistically refined. His use of a variety of verse meters is particularly praiseworthy. Of special note are the lyric moments in the songs of the dreamer, and the heroic tone of the flashbacks that relate the story of the past expedition. In the former, the verse form is usually short and the song is brief. In the latter, the verse is more narrative and prosaic with longer lines. Only rarely does this work suffer needless elaboration or dramatic lapses in the dialogue.

As is true in *Don Quijote*, and to some extent in *El fuego*, characterization in this drama is not overly problematical because Ríos again depends on universal models. The Captain is distinguished from Jason only by his human lust and emotional foibles. The Princess helps deliver the Captain from danger in practically the same manner that her classical model, Medea, delivered Jason. Both women, for example, butchered their brother's body and scattered the pieces for their fathers to find. The Princess is a faithful imitation of Medea until the end of the drama when she kills her sons and herself.

The boys are not of Ríos' creation, either, because they have acknowledged models to be found in the legend of Medea. Both are rather flat characters, and their basic importance is twofold: to substantiate succeeding plot development and the character portrayals of the Princess and the Captain and to inject a note of social interest in *La selva*. In this latter regard, their arguments early in the first act expose the Conquest's concern with the new mestizo elements in the predominantly Spanish and Indian population. The eight-year-old is critical of his Indian mother, whom he blames for his mestizo heritage, and respects his father as a hero. The feelings of the ten year old are reversed. He loves his mother more deeply and believes his father to be guilty of some mysterious crime which has forced the family to a fugitive existence. In terms of an extended social commentary, the boys' views also may be construed as opposing archetypal reactions when considered in an anthropological and sociohistorical context: that of the conquered (Indian) and that of the conqueror (Spaniard). In this light, Ríos has only incorporated into his drama an issue with which innumerable writers, such as the Inca Garcilaso and the late José María Arguedas, have contended. Regardless of their interpretations, Ríos' social implications in *La selva* are kept at a low level. More than stamping the work with a genuine social concern, the use of economic and racial class differences is included to "Americanize" the drama and is frequent in the author's production.

There are other themes besides the social one mentioned above. In addition to the dust-to-dust theme, there is the customary dramatization of personal agony based on hatred and followed by death as the final escape. This work is also characteristic of Ríos' works in that it is not an action-packed creation, but one which is ideological in its appeal. In conclusion, *La selva* is Ríos' outstanding composition in practically every respect. It is substantial evidence that its author has been unjustly overlooked as one of the three most important dramatists of contemporary Peru.

Most generations in Peru have produced a drama dealing with some aspect of the Inca empire. *Ayar Manko*[11] is the best contribution of Ríos' generation and, as such, won the 1952 Premio Nacional de Teatro. In his preface to this drama the author asserts that it is not meant to be an historical reconstruction. Nevertheless, the work does have a factual basis. José Hesse Murga, in his introduction to *Teatro peruano contemporáneo*, points out that the drama was inspired by Fernández de Oviedo's *Historia de los Incas*, Pedro Sarmiento de Gamboa's *Historia de los Incas*, Garcilaso de la Vega el Inca's *Comentarios reales de los Incas*, Luis Alberto Sánchez' *Historia de America*, and Cristóbal de Molina's *Fábulas y ritos de los Incas*.[12] Ríos' drama is the story of Ayar Manko's struggle to overcome fraternal jealousies and envy before assuming the royal crown of Tampu Toko. This is but one episode, then, in the pre-Columbian history of the Inca empire.

The play begins with a conflict. The King is dying and must choose a successor from among his four sons: Auka, Uchu, Manko, and Achi. Achi is selected, but dies in a landslide before his coronation, and the covetous Auka surreptitiously usurps the throne. He is immediately beset by frustrating calamities and growing opposition to his leadership, and retaliates with a reign of terror. By the third act Auka's frustration has turned to agony because the calamities have continued and Manko is the popular favorite to replace him. It is apparent that Auka's ambition and envy, coupled with his hatred of Manko, have become the tools of his own destruction. His reign of terror has created a kingdom of death from which he can find no escape. In the final cuadro, Manko takes the crown for himself and Auka, seeing his every ambition broken, throws himself over a precipice to end his agony. Death becomes the only escape from his kingdom of death.

Ríos generally develops one major character in each work to be the embodiment of his dramatic themes. This is true in *Don Quijote*, *Los bufones*, *El fuego*, *El reino sobre las tumbas*, and also in *Ayar Manko*. Auka is the most fully developed character and dominates the work. There is little to add to the discussion of Ríos' dramatic themes as seen in this character. Auka is the usual agonized ruler of a kingdom of death, and his only escape from his self-wrought agony is death. His frustrated ambition is the principal motivating factor of his hate. He is distinguished from the author's other protagonists only by the unusual emphasis on his envy, which results from his frustrated ambitions. It should be noticed that Auka seeks only to sate his greed and that the use of a personal dream, as it is usually included in Ríos' dramas, is absent.

Manko is ostensibly a stereotyped personage, a symbol of the noble, loyal, and just ideal. His actions are more readily predictable than Auka's because he is a typed character. Uchu and Wako, the wife of Achi, are also secondary

11. Juan Ríos, *Ayar Manko*, pp. 95-182, in *Teatro peruano contemporáneo*, ed. José Hesse Murga (Madrid: Aguilar, 1963).

12. *Ibid.*, 18.

characters, yet their presence lends considerable substance to the dramatic involvement and complications. Their opposition to Auka, for instance, is indispensable in formulating the frustration that characterizes the ruler and leads to his suicide.

While there is nothing novel in the structural arrangement of *Ayar Manko*, it is exemplary of Ríos' artistic sense of balance and his dramatic equilibrium. Each act is a story in itself, for each has a beginning and an end, and each is, at the same time, an integral part of the whole. For example, the twofold division of Act III is meant, in the first cuadro, to reinforce Auka's inability to end his agony during the two years that have passed since Act II. The second contains the denouement and final take-over by the noble Manko.

In his preface to this drama, Ríos also states that he intended the aesthetic to overshadow the realistic appeal, and for the symbol to be more important than the anecdote. In the main, he accomplished what he set out to do, but the aesthetic appeal is marred somewhat by an overemphasis on philosophic digressions and by rhetorical repetition. As in several dramas by Ríos, the dialogues in *Ayar Manko* are not always natural in tone or progression, and they are often overextended. Ríos apparently is aware of his verbosity since those sections to be suppressed for stage presentation are marked by an *X* and, as he suggests, may also be omitted by the reader. This criticism is not to deny that Ríos has few, if any, peers who can equal his lyric capabilities as a dramatist. A good indication of this is the song and ballet that end Act II. This brief interlude is interpolated skillfully and is a well-timed relief from the tense moment that precedes. Its omission would rob *Ayar Manko* of its highest lyric moment. More importantly, this ballet scene, which dramatizes the official condemnation of Auka's acts, is a necessary link in the development of the drama.

In summary, *Ayar Manko* is an indispensable addition to Ríos' repertory. The delineation of the secondary characters and the structural merits are the outstanding features of the play. And, even though there are a few dark moments aesthetically, it is a solid and appealing treatment of a tragedy of universal, especially Hispanic, renown.

El mar,[13] the seventh drama presented by Ríos, written in free verse and divided into seven cuadros, debuted in Lima in 1954. Like *El fuego*, El reino *sobre las tumbas*, and *La selva*, *El mar* reflects Ríos' inspirational indebtedness to the classical antiquities. In the "Explicación necesaria," which prefaces the work, he acknowledges that *El mar* is an adaptation of the *Oresteia* to the coast of Peru. As such, the work begins with an exposé of the love affair that has developed between Egidio and Clara after the supposed death at sea of her husband, Agustín. Clara's children, Elsa and Orlando, oppose their adulterous relationship and do not believe their father is dead.

When Agustín does return, he is murdered in a manner which recalls the death of Agamemnon by Clytemnestra. He is ensnared in a net and slaughtered with his own axe by Egidio and Clara. When Elsa discovers his body, she

13. Juan Ríos, *El Mar*, mimeographed (Lima: Compañía Lucía Irurita, 1954).

vows that she and Orlando will avenge the crime. She subsequently lures Egidio so that Orlando can stab him to death. In the final cuadro, Clara comes in answer to her lover's cries and meets the same fate at the hand of her son. Vengeance does not prove to be a meaningful reward for Elsa and Orlando, however. They realize that they have perpetuated the destruction and hatred they once abhorred, and that death is the only escape from its agony. Their last act is to commit suicide in the sea, a symbol of the life-giving source and, at the same time, their only salvation from life.

The most striking feature of *El mar* is the manner in which it closely parallels the classic legends in the *Oresteia*. Even the names of the characters suggest that Ríos has derived them from the classical figures: Clytemnestra is now Clara, Aegisthus is Egidio, Electra is Elsa, and Orestes is Orlando. Of course, as the preceding synopsis suggests, the similarities between the characters of the legends and those of the drama are more extensive. For the purpose of this discussion, however, it should be pointed out that Ríos' personages are not fully developed characters. They scarcely go beyond a simple identity with the epic and legendary traits of their models. Ríos' only purpose here is to emphasize those personal characteristics which he can relate to his favorite thematic interests. The story of Clara, for example, affords an easy opportunity to dramatize how remorse is perpetuated by hatred and destruction. Clara is the first to create a kingdom of death, and, as with so many of Ríos' characters, death is the only certain escape from her agony. This point is reiterated when Elsa and Orlando murder Clara and Egidio and immediately recognize the consequence of their vengeance. They know that they have only replaced Clara and Egidio as those responsible for maintaining the village under a veil of death. Unlike their legendary models, however, Elsa and Orlando realize there is no escape from their worldly existence and they commit suicide.

El mar, then, defends Ríos' attitude that man cannot escape his fatal destiny, and, in this tragedy at least, the author unmistakably relates man's destiny with his immediate surroundings. For this reason, he appropriately employs the type of language and setting which best reinforce the fatalistic and naturalistic aspects of *El mar*. The language, for instance, is a convincing imitation of the vernacular used by the poorer members of Peru's fishing villages. Yet, as Ríos points out in the "Explicación necesaria," this language is not in support of any regional interest: "Me parecía difícil emplear el idioma de nuestros pescadores sin menoscabo de la dignidad—o a la inversa usar el lenguaje culto sin caer en el artificio literario. Luego de larga reflexión, decidí sacrificar la correción gramatical en aras de la naturalidad. Pero no está de más aclarar que en ningún monento he buscado el 'color local.' Me he limitado a adaptar, al ritmo de verso suelto, la manera de hablar de nuestro pueblo." By choosing a fishing village for the setting, Ríos visually supports the poverty of his characters as well as the real and symbolic influence of nature on their existence. Justifying also his choice of setting, Ríos writes that "hace algunos años me sentí tentado por la idea de trasplantar—humilde y respetuosamente—'La Orestiada' a la costa del Perú. El árido y grandioso paisaje del litoral ofrece un escenario adecuado para la modernización del viejo mito." The implication, of course, is that the sterile and deserted environs of the Peruvian coast, thus the village, are a natural complement to the stark and lugubrious story of his drama.

Despite the obvious parallels that exist between *El mar* and its classical model, this drama is not a denial of Ríos' artistic originality. Instead, it is additional proof that one of the author's principal merits as a dramatist is his ability to adapt the classics to works of modern design and audience appeal. His use of language and the setting of *El mar*, in combination with characters derived from universal classical models, substantiate Ríos' mastery of the genre.

Los desesperados,[14] a three-act drama in prose, was written in 1951 and revised in 1960. The work is Ríos' single drama of twentieth-century design and has no acknowledged classical source. As will be seen, nonetheless, the play is reminiscent of Ríos' second drama, *El fuego*. Both have an American setting and reflect a revolutionary optimism founded in the patriotic sensibilities of their respective protagonists.

This, Ríos' last work, centers on Luciano, a revolutionary terrorist, who believes that only an aggressive attitude can effectively challenge the social injustices to which his nation is subjected. To initiate the rebels' coup d'état, he assigns Daniel to murder a general. The second act portrays the psychological effect the murder has on Daniel. He is ultimately captured and tortured to betray his cause, but the physical suffering gives him reason to consider himself a martyr. The last act again focuses on Luciano and the coup d'état he has instigated. As the play ends, the remaining rebel forces are surrounded and face certain defeat. Yet Luciano, ever true to his rebel cause, refuses to surrender, preferring to meet the enemy alone if necessary.

Los desesperados offers little in the way of structural novelty. In fact, the play only reflects Ríos' traditional use of the first act to introduce the players, with the second and third acts containing the usual complication and denouement. It is also true that the drama is typical of Ríos in that the dramatic conflict is of an inner and personal nature, and not dependent on real action to assure its acceptance.

Stylistically, however, this play is a unique experience in the trajectory of Ríos' production. It proves that he is not bound to creating poetic drama. In fact, the change in form here is made so skillfully that it seems as if the author had always composed in prose and is unaware of his poetic capabilities. The expression of Ríos' usual themes in prose also suggests that *Los desesperados* represents a move away from works with heroic and epic overtones and inspired in classical myth and legend.

Another important change in technique is seen in the manner in which the themes are dramatized. Ríos usually portrays an individual whose dream, whatever it is, perpetuates his agonized existence. Hate and death maintain the individual's torment and his dream is to escape his own existence. Death, ironically, is the only escape. *Los desesperados* departs from this tendency inasmuch

14. Ríos, *Los desesperados*, pp. 527-649, in *Teatro* by Ríos.

as no single character embodies all these thematic implications. It is also noteworthy that no character has a true dream that he seeks to fulfill. In each case, the motivating factor on the personal level is better described as dedication or ambition.

For example, Luciano, the principal character, is not of heroic or epic proportions. He never possesses the Promethean qualities of the once compassionate and idealistic Captain in *El fuego*. From the beginning, Luciano is an uncompromising revolutionary aware that he is no more than a human element in a real world. It would be farfetched to assert that Luciano, as the Captain, is motivated by a dream of martyrdom and that he is vainglorious. He is only an individual totally dedicated to the party's cause. In sum, Luciano is a credible character, not an obvious dramatization of the heroic ideal. An audience would possibly identify with Luciano, but not with the more symbolic Captain.

Daniel, the secondary character of importance in *Los desesperados*, is the author's thematic representation of the tortured individual who suffers the agony of the reign of death and hate. Daniel is reminiscent of Auka in *Ayar Manko* because both men's criminal acts isolate them from their surrounding society. Nevertheless, Daniel has no dream or dedication. He seems to be more loyal to the party members than dedicated to any party cause. The plight of Daniel, as portrayed in the entire second act, is included to give dramatic and thematic substance to the play. Without his story, only a skeletal framework would remain, and Luciano's role in the first and third acts would be so weak as to be insignificant.

Xavier, another secondary character who appears in the second act, is likewise included to dramatize another of Ríos' customary themes. He is the agonized man who, after being captured with Daniel, severely suffers the effect of hate and destruction. Xavier has neither true loyalty, dedication, nor a dream to help him endure his existence, however, and he commits suicide to terminate his misery.

Ríos' reason for distributing the thematic interpretations and implications among several characters is not clear. One possibility is that by doing so he intended to refine his dramatic technique and lend depth to a greater number of characters. This is accomplished partially, but it also must be noted that no single character is fully developed. Neither Daniel nor Luciano is as fully developed as Auka in *Ayar Manko*, the Captain in *El fuego*, or the Captain in *La selva*. One other reason for this thematic distribution may have been the desire to avoid overextended dialogue for any one character, something that is clearly evident in Ríos' earlier works. If these are the reasons, then the thematic distribution among several characters is justifiable and significant.

There are secondary aspects of *Los desesperados* that substantiate its dramatic appeal more than its thematic significance. One is a romance between two of the younger rebels, and another is the almost secret love Luciano has for the mother of Xavier. A third is a slight social concern similar to that in *El fuego*. It is based on the economic and racial class distinctions existing in Latin American society since the Independence Period. This concern is the principal motivation factor in the rebels' revolutionary effort, but its actual dramatization is weak because it stems from social inequality, a condition which the audience accepts *a priori*. Finally, the social note strengthens the author's effort to "Americanize" the drama.

Los desesperados is unique among the dramas by Juan Ríos. Its style and tone of revolutionary optimism clearly distinguish it from his other creations. Neither is it typical insofar as its thematic contents and characterizations are concerned. The changes in this drama suggest that Ríos had begun to alter his standard dramatic formula to one which would overcome some of his technical weaknesses, such as rhetorical repetition, poetic stagnation, and the tendency to philosophize. It is the last of his dramas, and, in my opinion, second only to *La selva*.

It is unfortunate that Juan Ríos has not presented any new plays since 1960. Nonetheless, his production is to be recognized as an important stimulus to the theatrical renaissance in Peru which began a little more than twenty-five years ago. Ríos is an eclectic who blends poetic, heroic, American, and even philosophical elements to produce a drama that surmounts the obstacles of national interests that have restricted so many of his compatriots. For example, his initial creation as a dramatist, *Don Quijote*, has been successful in Spain, and *Ayar Manko* is known in several Hispanic-American countries.

Ríos' drama is of a personal nature, yet none of his works is truly psychological. The characters may be modeled after Jason, Prometheus, or Philip IV of Spain, but they are never completely developed. Neither is the characterization of the principal personage appreciably altered in the different plays: he is a transcendental being who embodies Ríos' concern for the agonized individual in a society perpetuated by acts of death and hate. If these acts cease, however, the individual's existence is terminated. Death, then, is the only salvation from worldly existence. As a consequence, all of these characters attempt to fulfill a utopian dream or ambition, and one of the most frequent of these is the establishment of a society devoid of hate and injustice. The irony and basic conflict is that forces of destruction are usually released in the fulfillment of these dreams and ambitions.

There are other elements in Ríos' works frequently woven into the overall dramatic fiber to blend homogeneously with the shades of despair and agony. One is the inevitability of death and the accompanying dust-to-dust theme. Another is reminiscent of the concept that we are all dreamed by a Superior Being and when His dream ends we cease to exist and return to nothingness. Ríos is not an existentialist, nor is he an escapist. But the suggestion of his personal interest in writers of this ilk cannot be overlooked entirely, as evidenced by the frequent pessimistic, agonizing, and fatalistic moments to be found throughout his production. Yet another element found in his works is the dramatization of Hispano-American social and ethnic problems. This is accomplished by emphasizing racial and economic class distinctions and problems of the mestizo in society.

Ríos tends to write his drama in long narrative verse with an epic overtone. Occasionally, he utilizes shorter lyric forms, and not uncommon is his predilection for combining song and dance. With regard to the latter, he favors the more aesthetically involved movements of ballet rather than those of simple folklore dances. Despite his lyric capabilities, the use of a variety of verse forms, and occasional moments of dramatic relief, however, Ríos has not been able to escape his stylistic repetitiveness and his propensity for poetic stagnation. These are his major dramatic weaknesses and are rooted in his tendency to be verbose.

Ríos' drama always has a strong structural foundation, and its division is meaningful and necessary. In some works, the traditional three acts are the only dividing line in the linear progression. In others, cuadros are used alone, or are used to subdivide the action. Regardless of the manner in which the cuadros are employed, their effect is to denote the episodic nature of the action. *Don Quijote* is an excellent example of how Ríos uses the brief segment effectively. It should be mentioned, also, that his works are accompanied by complete, and sometimes demanding, set directions. Ríos knows exactly what kind of scenic designs will complement his composition, and takes pains to formulate a precise description.

The most striking feature of Ríos' production is his extensive reliance on classical sources. Of the eight dramas herein discussed, *El reino sobre las tumbas*, *La selva*, *El fuego*, and *El mar* are directly based on classical myth or legend. And of the remaining four, only *Los desesperados* does not have a specified source of inspiration. While it is naturally difficult to explain or justify an author's inspirational indebtedness, one cannot escape the impression that Ríos well might have turned to new and different sources during his fifteen years as a dramatist. In this way he might have broadened his audience appeal, incorporated considerable originality into his writing, and extended his productivity in a significant direction. It is also feasible to assert that *Los desesperados* does indeed mark Ríos' break with his standard and poetic formula for composing drama. If he were to return as a dramatist, then, this play might prove to be his first step toward a renewal of his own dramaturgy.

In conclusion, Juan Ríos is a conservative dramatist who has been able to combine successfully the classic and the modern, reality and dream, and hope and despair in works which have been applauded by the Peruvian public for years. It is certain that any new plays he might write will meet an enthusiastic, hopefully enlarged audience which has missed his participation in the national theatre during the past fifteen years. Yet, regardless of his future activity as a playwright, Ríos' existing contributions to Peru's theatre will never be denied.

Within months after Juan Ríos had made his triumphant debut on the national stage, Sebastián Salazar Bondy equalled his feat with the premiere of *Amor, Gran laberinto*, his first dramatic creation, and thus began a period of production that was to span almost twenty years, some five years longer than that of Ríos, and which was terminated with his death in 1965. While the careers of these two writers developed simultaneously within the same city for more than a decade, their personal interests and approaches to drama could hardly be more divergent. Ríos, as we have seen, intently pursued his universal, often classical inspirations, within a framework of poetic tradition and structural and thematic unity. After his debut, on the other hand, Salazar set out to create a theatre which, while characterized by its realistic, even national, limitations, was consistently in a state of experimental change. Despite his efforts and considerable national recognition as a dramatist, Salazar remained relatively unknown outside Peru until after his death. Since then, his international reputation has justifiably increased, and now there is little doubt that no one since Manuel Asencio Segura (1806-1871) has been able to match Salazar's achievements and contributions to the Peruvian theatre.

Salazar was born in Lima in 1924, and in 1938 his first verses were published in his high school magazine. Just six years later, while a student at the University of San Marcos, he began his professional career with the publication of two collections of verse, *Rótulo de la esfinge* (1943) and *Bahía del dolor* (1943). Before the end of the Second World War, a number of his short stories and literary essays had appeared in local newspapers and literary magazines. Then, in 1946, Salazar made his debut as a dramatist in Lima with the presentation of *Amor, Gran laberinto.* That same year, he married the Argentine actress Inda Ledesma and from 1948 to 1950 lived in Buenos Aires as a correspondent for *La nación*, one of that capital's foremost dailies. Salazar returned to Lima in 1950 and by 1955 had firmly established himself as a prominent dramatist with a number of successful plays: in 1950, he wrote *La soltera y el ladrón* and *La oficina del Arlequín*, both brief one-act works, and *Como vienen se van*, which was revised as *Dos viejas van por la calle* in 1959; and in 1952, he won the Premio Nacional de Teatro for *Rodil*, a three-act historical drama. These plays were followed by a reworking of the Peruvian classic *Ollantay*, done in collaboration with César Miró Quesada in 1953; several of his best known one-act pieces, such as *El de la valija* (1953), *El espejo no hace milagros* (1953), and *En el cielo no hay petróleo* (1954); and *No hay isla feliz* (1954), a social drama in three acts.

In 1956, Salazar received a scholarship given by the French government to study in the Conservatoire National d'Arte in Paris. From this brief experience, he was impressed by the vitality of the French vaudeville and boulevard theatres and, especially, by their popular, satirical, and local elements. Of secondary interest to him was the popular operetta, with its choreographic and lyric appeal. The period following Salazar's return to Lima in 1956 was a transitional one, as he began to depart from his earlier realistic social drama, such as *No hay isla feliz*, toward a satirical costumbrista creation tempered by the addition of colorful criollo elements. In this new stage of development, he was still concerned with the social problems in Peru, but his condemnation on stage was not as bitter as before. Works representative of this change of interest are the one-act comedy *Un cierto tic tac* (1956) and Salazar's second social drama, *Algo que quiere morir* (1956).

Salazar was fomenting popular interest in the national theatre even before the 1960's. He began to combine his refined skills and new interests, such as those he gathered in France, to produce a theatre that was more modern and appealing, yet still local in nature. As a result, his drama became more impartial socially, almost concessive, with simple conflicts and sensational solutions. With only one exception, that being *Flora Tristán* (1956), an historical estampa, the characters in his plays continued to be types which were ostensibly local in their speech, outward appearance, and social reactions. In fact, Salazar's plays during these years, from 1958 to 1965, are reminiscent of the nineteenth-century costumbrista works as written by Segura, yet they still maintained a direct relation with twentieth-century Peruvian society by way of their contemporary interests. Those works that are most representative of the changes which Salazar introduced are *Dos viejas van por la calle* (1959), *El fabricante de deudas* (1962), and *La escuela de los chismes* (1965), a three-act thesis drama.

In the early 1960's Salazar's political and nontheatrical involvements increased, and he temporarily curtailed his dramatic production. During 1960, for instance, he was invited to visit China, spent a brief time in Moscow, was awarded the Premio León de Greiff for poetry in Caracas and the annual Premio Cabotín as the outstanding journalist in Lima, and finished his book on the various artistic expressions in Peru, *Del hueso tallado al arte abstracto.* Two years later, *El fabricante de deudas*, a three-act drama, premiered in Lima and was awarded the important Premio Anita Fernandini de Naranjo as the best Peruvian drama of the year. Salazar also travelled to Havana in 1962 as a drama critic for Casa de las Américas. Upon his return to Lima, he was appointed a representative for his political party, La Frente Democrática Nacional, and devoted considerable time to the fulfillment of this obligation.

Salazar's interest in the theatre again quickened in the latter years of his life, and, despite his other activities, he travelled to Japan, where he was invited to study the theatrical situation in that country. By the early months of 1965, Salazar's health was failing rapidly, yet his energies were still directed toward the theatre in Peru. He aided in the production of *La escuela de los chismes*; wrote his first musical comedy, *Ifigenia en el mercado*; and put the finishing touches to *El Rabdomante*, a one-act drama which was awarded the 1965 Premio Nacional de Teatro, his third. Salazar was composing *El tacto de la araña* (1966), a collection of verse, when he died on 4 July 1965, from the effects of a recurrent hepatic ailment that had affected his health for several years.

Shortly after Salazar's death, Peru's playwrights and theatre critics began to assess the significance of their loss. They realized that the national theatre had lost not only an able counselor, director, and producer, but also its most accomplished dramatist. Particularly painful for many was the fact that there was no immediate hope that Salazar's vacancy would be filled. The situation was especially threatening to the recent, and still unstable, spirit of theatrical renewal that had begun shortly before 1950. As late as 1976, this state of uncertainty prevails.[15]

15. For further discussion of the present day Peruvian theatre, see Daniel R. Reedy and Robert J. Morris, "The Lima Theatre, 1966-67," *Latin American Theatre Review*, 1(Fall 1967):26-38.

Salazar's total dramatic production is comprised of ten major works and eleven brief, one-act pieces. The first of these minor works is *Los novios*, which was written in 1947, shortly after the premiere of *Amor, Gran laberinto*. Salazar assigned his short pieces a variety of names, such as juego, juguete, and mojiganga, but they are all similar in the farcical atmosphere, the portrayal of Pirandellian characters, the mixture of tragedy and comedy, their thematic universality, and the absence of a refined, artificial language. Like Salazar's longer plays, the short works are of an uneven quality, with some of them being noticeably superior to others. Unlike the longer compositions, on the other hand, they are not generally limited by costumbrista or by regionalistic elements.

Amor, Gran laberinto[16] represents Salazar's first step towards a career in the theatre and, as such, was an enviable success because it brought him Peru's second annual Premio Nacional de Teatro in 1947. It is a poetic farce divided into two acts and an epilogue and is written in a prose reminiscent of Spain's eighteenth-century drama. The obvious theme suggested by the title would seem to be the danger of man's reason being incapacitated by passion, namely love; yet in the preface, Salazar asserted that his true theme and purpose was to satirize man and his social institutions. It is a benign satire, nonetheless, because the farce demonstrates faith in man and society.

Amor, Gran laberinto also is a distortion of a social reality that is at times comic and grotesque. This distortion, in combination with the puppetlike characters and the fantastic atmosphere which prevails, suggests the possible influence of various authors such as Valle-Inclán and García Lorca. On the other hand, there seems to be no real influence (excepting titular similarity and implied thematic interpretations) from Sor Juana Inés' seventeenth-century drama, *Amor es más laberinto*.

Despite the initial success of *Amor, Gran laberinto*, it is not a reliable indication of the skills and interests which Salazar was to display later on. One criticism that can be leveled against the farce is the poor handling of the dialogues. They are frequently artificial and stilted or riddled with exaggerated archaic constructions that fail to complement the baroque atmosphere. Yet, in all fairness, and without denial of this weakness, Salazar's first drama is an intensely dramatic composition, and among his other works there is no better example of his artistic sensitivity.

Rodil[17] is Salazar's first three-act drama, but more importantly, it is the first of his realistic and regionalistic works. It also was awarded the 1952 Premio Nacional de Teatro. Specifically, *Rodil* is an historical drama that indirectly eulogizes the Peruvian independence movement by emphasizing the efforts of Rodil, a Spanish military officer, and of his command to resist the nationalistic siege of Fort Real Felipe in Callao. Salazar based much of the drama on factual information culled from the diary kept by Commander José Ramón Rodil

16. Sebastián Salazar Bondy, *Amor, Gran laberinto*, pp. 251-322, in *Teatro peruano contemporáneo*, ed. Aurelio Miró Quesada (Lima: Editorial Huascarán, 1948).

17. Sebastián Salazar Bondy, *Rodil*, pp. 7-61, in *Teatro* by Salazar (Buenos Aires: Editorial Losada, 1961).

throughout the siege, which lasted from 9 December 1824 to 22 January 1826.[18] The fictitious characterization of Rodil, however, was apparently inspired by that of the protagonist in Ricardo Palma's *Rodil* (1852). Palma's drama is of the usual Romantic fare, somewhat sensational emotionally, and has practically no historical relation with the Peruvian independence movement. This latter work, incidentally, was never produced, and was unknown until 1952,[19] the same year in which Salazar's *Rodil* was first staged in Lima. But regardless of Salazar's probable source of inspiration, his portrayal of Rodil is unquestionably superior to Palma's.

In *Rodil*, Salazar made marked improvement with regard to his manipulation of language and dialogue. Because his purpose was to compose a realistic historical drama, he wisely abandoned the artificial poetic anachronisms of *Amor, Gran laberinto* and resorted to the natural and spontaneous expressions which the work demanded. Only in this way could he assure a convincing reenactment of the siege and a penetrating portrayal of Rodil's character. *Rodil* is one of Salazar's most evenly balanced and carefully structured creations, and it is particularly admirable for the skillful superimposition of fact over fiction.

No hay isla feliz[20] is Salazar's first major social drama, and was premiered in Lima in 1954. It is divided into three acts, with the first and third acts composed of two *cuadros* each and, like all of Salazar's dramatic pieces, is in prose. The drama was apparently written with the Peruvian public in mind, because it is the first work in which Salazar specified his personal concern for the social welfare of his people, particularly the emerging middle class. As a result, foreign interest in the work is severely restricted by insistence on certain regionalistic elements such as dialectal variants, local setting, characterizations, and, especially, social preoccupations.

Like many of Salazar's compositions, this work is based, in part, on fact. A few years prior to the writing of this play, the Peruvian government altered its plan to build a highway extension through an undisclosed southern coastal village,[21] and this drama is a fictitious version of the manner in which this change of plans shattered the dreams of the villagers. Specifically, Salazar elaborated on the factual base in his original portrayal of a family conflict meant to symbolize the modern social crisis in Peru. He plainly suggests that the Peruvian people must struggle against awesome forces, even against their own government and prejudices at times, if they are to achieve a higher social and economic level of existence.

In addition to certain artistic limitations, *No hay isla feliz* is weak technically due to a disturbing vacillation in the dramatic progression of time and action. In turn, this fault in the basic structure of the play detracts from the desirable

18. José Ramón Rodil y Gayoso, *La defensa del Callao por don José Ramón Rodil durante el periodo comprendido entre la capitulación de Ayacucho y el embarque en la* Britón (Madrid: Imprenta Palomeque, 1930).

19. José Jiménez Borja, "Un hallazgo inesperado," *Mar del sur*, 23 (septiembre-octubre 1952):34.

20. Salazar, *No hay isla feliz*, pp. 63-119, in *Teatro* by Salazar.

21. José Miguel Oviedo, "Sebastián Salazar Bondy en su teatro," *Revista Peruana de Cultura*, 7-8(junio 1966):88.

fluidity in the thematic development of the work. Despite the fact that this play is not exemplary of Salazar's usual artistic standards, it is valuable because it clearly exposes his concern with the national social dilemma. Within a few years after the release of this work, Salazar's political interests, as expressed in his drama, were to become more liberal, if not radical, to many of his compatriots. In this regard, *No hay isla feliz* was an impressive initial statement.

Salazar continued his presentation of contemporary middle-class problems in Peru with *Algo que quiere morir*,[22] a three-act drama premiered in Lima in 1956. In this work he focused on several manifestations of the so-called generation gap, a sociological phenomenon which he related to man's innate egotism and selfishness. The drama concerns the manner in which three middle-class children remain wayward and unwilling to accept the traditional values of their parents until, when matured, they fail to attain their exaggerated youthful goals and expectations.

Thematically, the play offers nothing new, and, as *No hay isla feliz*, its appeal is somewhat restricted to the Peruvian audience due to its costumbrista and nationalistic preoccupations. Technically, however, *Algo que quiere morir* is superior to the former work due to its streamlined, improved structure. It is not bound by Salazar's usual episodic arrangement, and there is a noticeable absence of those extraneous elements which frequently blemished some of his best works. Despite its few technical improvements, *Algo que quiere morir* should not be overly praised. It has won no awards and has not been staged for any significant length of time, in Lima or elsewhere, because it fails to sustain public interest.

Flora Tristán,[23] Salazar's second historical drama, is in three acts. It was written in 1958, premiered on a radio broadcast in Lima in 1959, and published in 1961 along with *Rodil*, *No hay isla feliz*, and *Algo que quiere morir*. The work is based on the life and political struggles of Flora Tristán, founder of the nineteenth-century Workers' Union in France.

The drama is not entirely a product of Salazar's imagination. He categorized the work as an estampa dramática and, in this case, the label denotes an attempt to dramatize facts without departing appreciably from historical truth and recorded documents. Yet while Salazar never formally acknowledged his factual sources, investigations have led me to the conclusion that they are twofold. The first consists of numerous biographical texts such as *Una mujer sola contra el mundo* by Luis Alberto Sánchez[24] and *Flora Tristán, Precursora* by Magda Portal.[25]

The second, and in all probability the source which proved most valuable to Salazar, is *Peregrinaciones de una paria*, translated by Luis Alberto Sánchez in 1941 from the original, *Peregrinations d'une paria*, written in 1837 by Flora Tristán. This book is a record of her impressions and experiences during a trip

22. Salazar, *Algo que quiere morir*, pp. 121-179, in *Teatro* by Salazar.
23. Salazar, *Flora Tristán*, pp. 181-216, in *Teatro* by Salazar.
24. Luis Alberto Sánchez, *Una mujer sola contra el mundo* (Buenos Aires: n.p., 1937).
25. Magda Portal, *Flora Tristán, Precursora* (Santiago: n.p., 1944).

to South America in 1833 and 1834. The dramatist probably was also influenced to some extent by *L'Union Ouvrière*, a pamphlet in which Flora Tristán outlined her sociopolitical considerations.

Salazar apparently intended the work to be a succinct dramatization of Flora Tristán's personal struggles and, for this reason, refrained from including extraneous characters and events. In fact, there is practically no action on stage, and each act is simply a dialogue between Flora Tristán and one other person, each of whom represents an important period of her life. In contrast with Salazar's previous dramas, the language used in this work is concise and unencumbered by regionalisms. It is also worthy of note that, as a result of the absence of action and the exclusive dependence on dialogue, this play is as meaningful when read as when viewed on stage. For the first time in his career, Salazar's use of language is the focal point of his dramatic, as well as his artistic, expression.

Flora Tristán does not merit an award for creative excellence. The estampa is, to a considerable extent, simply a recapitulation of documented sources and Salazar made no attempt to disguise the work as an entirely original composition. He obviously depended on, and adapted his sources of material to reflect, as accurately as possible, the content of Flora Tristán's two most influential publications, *Peregrinations d'une paria* and *L'Union Ouvrière*. In this regard, the similarity between the previously existing sources and the dramatic creation is justifiable.

Dos viejas van por la calle[26] was first presented by the theatrical group Histrión in Lima in 1959. The play is historically important because it marks Salazar's departure from his previously realistic orientation towards an emphasis on satiric costumbrista elements. The works written during this, his third stage of development, are reminiscent of the nineteenth-century theatre in Lima, particularly of the criollo drama as written by Manuel Asencio Segura.

It has been mentioned before that *Dos viejas van por la calle* is a revision of *Como vienen se van*, which Salazar wrote in 1950. He was apparently dissatisfied with his original artistic treatment of the play and never released it for presentation. He was, however, convinced of the dramatic possibilities of the initial version and, in the late 1950's, decided to rework it as an expression of his new dramatic interests. As it is now published, the play consists of a prologue, three short acts, and an epilogue. It concerns the efforts of two elderly spinster sisters to mold and influence their young adopted nephew so that he will reflect their own traditional social standards. Their tragic failure is ultimately due to their own hypocrisy, their double standard of decency, and to the irresponsible attitude of modern society, which, as reflected in the actions of their nephew, they do not understand. The nephew is a pathetic character, weak and irresponsible. He is unwilling even to oppose his domineering bride and her avaricious demand that his two aunts be driven from the home.

26. Sebastián Salazar Bondy, *Dos viejan van por la calle*, pp. 201-262, in *Obras*, vol. 1 (Lima: n.p., 1967).

The events of these three acts take place in the past, but are structurally framed by the prologue and the epilogue, each of which is a brief moment in the present time. In the prologue the two ladies are seen passing through the streets of Lima to the place where they receive free food. They are destitute, and one is demented, as suggested by her repetitive speech patterns. In the epilogue, the sisters cross the stage going in the opposite direction. They have only one container of food because the demented sister accidentally spilled hers in the street. It is obvious now that their life is a miserable, degrading experience, and that they are totally dependent on charity for their existence.

The theme of this work is the ruinous effect wrought by hypocritical prejudice and greed. This social criticism, in combination with Salazar's caricaturesque portrayals and his costumbrista emphasis, is indicative of the extent to which this work parallels the satiric theatre of social intent as written in the latter half of the past century in Peru. *Dos viejas van por la calle*, however, is not one of Salazar's better compositions, and it is the least appealing of the plays which he wrote during his third stage of development. The major disadvantage of the play is the unconvincing manner in which the dramatic action and tension are developed in the three acts. This is, to a degree, a result of the poor, almost disruptive transition between the acts. The episodic nature of each act suggests that Salazar wrote three loosely knit costumbrista sketches and then attempted to endow them with a sense of dramatic unity and purpose by adding the prologue and the epilogue. Without this addition, however, the structural continuity would be even weaker, the dramatization of events would lose much of their satirical and dramatic appeal, and the thematic significance of the entire work would be seriously impaired.

This play does have a few redeeming features, which substantiate the reputation it still commands in Lima. Among these are Salazar's elaboration of and emphasis on those elements characteristic of Lima. The local speech peculiarities and social environment are foremost in this respect. Other factors of positive import are the simplicity of the plot, the rapid but lucid development of the dramatic action, and the originality with which Salazar has reworked an age-old theme.

As it was mentioned previously, Salazar's personal observations of the French theatre in 1956 eventually led to a stylistic change in his own dramas. *El fabricante de deudas*[27] is the first of his works to evidence the French influence, the first he purposely cast in a lighthearted mold, and the first of his works to include songs and intentional comic relief. Finally, the play is unique because, for the first time, Salazar avoided the somewhat bitter social denunciations characteristic of his previous works. Yet, even with these innovations, the work is of an obvious didactic nature, and is based on the popular adage that the love of money is the root of all evil. Salazar makes the true meaning of this wise counsel come to life in his portrayal of Obedot, a man whose very

27. Sebastián Salazar Bondy, *El fabricante de deudas. Flora Tristán* (Lima: Ediciones Nuevo Mundo, 1964), 8-87.

existence is regulated by both an insatiable thirst for material gain and the consequences of his own avaricious schemes.

Realistically, therefore, *El fabricante de deudas* does not represent a radical departure from Salazar's dramatic production up to 1963. For instance, the moral intentions, as found in *No hay isla feliz* and *Algo que quiere morir*, are also present here, the secondary characterizations are regionalistic archetypes, and this work is based on that of another writer. On the title page of the edition cited above, Salazar states that his play was inspired by Honoré de Balzac's short story *Le Faiseur*. Regardless of the debt to Balzac, Salazar's arrangement is deeply rooted in Peruvian tradition. In addition, the basic structure and many of the dramatic elements, primarily the dialogue and the description of local social customs, are reminiscent of the tenets defended in the earlier comedia costumbrista in Peru. Yet, while *El fabricante de deudas* is a reflection of the thesis drama of nineteenth-century Peru, as well as an unmistakable satire of modern Liman society, it has proven to be Salazar's most popular play among his compatriots.

La escuela de los chismes,[28] the third major composition of Salazar's period of satirical and costumbrista interests, was finished in 1963 and premiered in Lima in 1965. It was admittedly inspired by Richard Brinsley Sheridan's (1771-1816) *School for Scandal*, but, unfortunately, is a superficial, confusing, and lengthy (five long acts) adaptation of the famous original. Even Salazar's satirical attack on the baneful effects of gossip is weak and conventional.

The play is also structurally weak due to its overextension and, indirectly, to its story being obscured by the several secondary dramatic complications which have no bearing on the principal action current. Another weakness of note is that the language is inconsistent; it often is reduced to clichés, ready-made formulas, and other such linguistic crutches which seriously hamper the desirable naturalness and fluidity. Because there is little action on stage, this last weakness is especially acute in view of the fact that *La escuela de los chismes* depends heavily on the drawing room atmosphere and, particularly, the dialogues.

In comparison with most of Salazar's other works, the one in question is considerably more universal than regional in scope. There are, for example, few indications that the scene is laid in Lima, and there is a noticeable absence of Salazar's usual nationalistic social preoccupations. Because the characters are of a contemporary nature and represent the typical members of the middle class who have sufficient time to engage in noxious slander, the play is best judged a criticism of universal bourgeoise society. When considered on the basis of its artistic value, however, *La escuela de los chismes* is an ineffective creation, one which fails to project Salazar's capabilities as a polished dramatist.

The last work that Salazar wrote during his third period of development was *Ifigenia en el mercado*.[29] He finished the play during the early months of 1965,

28. Sebastián Salazar Bondy, *La escuela de los chismes*, mimeographed (Lima: Histrión, 1963).
29. Salazar, *Obras*, 1:407-458.

and it was premiered posthumously in 1966 in Lima by the theatrical group Compañía Lucía Irurita. This is Salazar's only musical comedy, yet he did not compose the musical scores. They were arranged by Enrique Iturriaga, one of Lima's better known song writers.

The entire piece is a lighthearted dramatization of the experiences of a young provincial girl in Lima. Ifigenia has come to live with her aunt in the market in order to escape the restrictive confines of a rural society. Like many new arrivals to the city, however, Ifigenia is unaware, even naive, of the pernicious intentions of the three men who romance her shortly after her arrival. A fourth man, a beggar, is also enamored of Ifigenia, yet his intentions are honorable and remain a secret until the final moments of the play. One of the first three men, a policeman, is the first to disappoint Ifigenia when he encarcerates his two opponents on exaggerated charges. His admitted purpose was to facilitate his pursuit of Ifigenia and to assure a promotion in rank. In the meantime, the beggar has won the lottery with a ticket that he found and gives his fortune to the unhappy Ifigenia so that she can bail the two men out of jail. The beggar realizes that she is distressed by the injustice dealt the two men. Once they are free, the two ingrates shun the beggar and reveal their dishonorable affections to Ifigenia. Then they flee the city to escape its treacherous society. Thus Ifigenia's faith in the benevolence of mankind is shattered. More devastating to her is the realization that the cosmopolitan society is not only more restrictive than that of the sierra, but is even inherently dangerous.

Ifigenia en el mercado has been one of Salazar's most successful costumbrista and satirical works. It has enjoyed a particularly favorable acceptance by the audiences in Lima. This popularity is due partially to the humorous and benign manner in which Salazar satirizes the life in the Capital city. A second justification of the success of the play lies in the author's elaboration of such local elements as the setting, a typical market area in Lima; the characters, essentially of the emergent middle class in cosmopolitan Peru; and the language, representatively Liman in its construction and spirit. Even the songs are traditional in the appeal to the audience in Lima.

Structurally, *Ifigenia en el mercado* is similar to Salazar's preceding major dramatic works, particularly those written since the late 1950's. Each of its four cuadros is episodic in nature, and each one offers a different vignette, or view, of the daily life of the ordinary inhabitant of Lima. The most important innovation, as suggested before, is the inclusion of two or more musical numbers in each division. These brief interludes serve a dual purpose. Technically they afford a lively and often humorous change of pace from the rapid development of the dramatic events. Secondly, Salazar took advantage of these interruptions to emphasize, though subtly, his thematic interests in the play. These are, principally, the social evils and weaknesses which Ifigenia's suitors represent, and her increasing discontent with the restrictions imposed by the urban society.

Salazar's ultimate motive for composing this musical comedy has been generally overlooked by his critics. For the majority of them the work is no more than an experimental deviation from his usual dramatic fare. When the play is viewed with regard to Salazar's entire dramatic production, however, it is much more significant. More than any other of his works, it then stands out as the climax towards reviving the theatre in Peru as a popular form of entertainment.

Shortly before his death in 1965, Salazar wrote an extended one-act play, *El Rabdomante*,[30] which is generally taken to be a renunciation of the popular, less serious theatre that he had perpetuated in the final years of his life. This play was an instant box office success in Lima and won the 1965 Premio Nacional de Teatro, awarded posthumously. If Salazar had lived, this work might have marked the definite beginning of a fourth stage of development in his career as a dramatist. More specifically, and with his last work as a hypothetical point of departure, it seems likely that the new stage would have been of a symbolic nature, with touches of the absurd tempered by a restrained criticism of social injustices. Yet, even though Salazar's new interests are suggested by *El Rabdomante*, it is also important to point out that the work can be construed as a refined fusion of the author's previously existing dramatic themes inasmuch as it contains the kind of social bitterness and condemnation found in his preceding works.

For those who are acquainted with any portion of Salazar's dramatic production, the composition and artistic effect of *El Rabdomante* are atypical. The work is unique for several reasons, not the least of which is that is does not have an acknowledged source of inspiration. It is more important that this work constitutes Salazar's first attempt to create Latin American drama, as opposed to one of restricted nationalistic proportions. He was able to avoid the limitations of nationalism because the problems he presents in *El Rabdomante* are not exclusively local in nature. Even the satirical tone is unique because it is more universal and vitriolic than in his other works. Finally, the absence of Salazar's usual costumbrista interests is marked by the avoidance of Peruvian speech peculiarities, dress, and setting.

El Rabdomante is also unique by way of the allegorization of such elements as the paramo, its inhabitants, their revolutionary tendencies, and even death, in order to emphasize social and personal ingratitude. At the same time, the dramatization of the futility of existence and of man's efforts to improve his lot suggests that Salazar was possibly leaning towards the more contemporary theatre of the absurd. This notion is strengthened by his personal interest in those contemporary French dramatists who have cultivated absurd and paradoxical elements in their own works.

In summary, *El Rabdomante* is the culmination of Salazar's total artistry. Also, it is his last play and most clearly substantiates the belief that his death was a serious blow to recent Peruvian efforts to improve the country's theatrical situation. One can only conjecture what the future would have brought if Salazar had lived to mature fully as a playwright.

30. Sebastián Salazar Bondy, *El Rabdomante*, mimeographed (Lima: Casa de la Cultura Peruana, 1965).

Salazar's principal dramatic works are based on a variety of themes and subject matter, which, as previously suggested, are intimately related to the different styles, or stages, of development he experienced during his eighteen-year career as a dramatist. The following comments are intended to make further distinctions in the four stages of Salazar's dramatic production and to support the concluding remarks on his overall importance to the Peruvian theatre.

The first stage of development is essentially a poetic one in which Salazar combined somber, satirical, and sometimes grotesque elements. His sociopolitical comments are somewhat caustic during this period, yet they are also of general intent and free of any nationalistic prejudice. Of his major works, only *Amor, Gran laberinto* falls entirely into this initial stage; probably because Salazar was just beginning to realize his own interests and capabilities as a dramatist. For this same reason, he rapidly passed into his second stage shortly after the premiere of this first work. Nonetheless, many of the sociopolitical interests and dramatic techniques he espoused in *Amor, Gran laberinto* were not forsaken and later reappeared in other dramas. For instance, Salazar's satirical vein and his intention to expose social foibles form the allegorical basis of *El Rabdomante.*

A marked interest in the national scene is the salient theme of Salazar's second stage of development. In the works of this period, the middle 1950's, his satirical attack on national problems is more poignant, but not as bitter. It is also during this period that Salazar became known as an articulate spokesman for the masses, particularly the emerging middle class, with such works as *No hay isla feliz* and *Algo que quiere morir.*

By the end of the 1950's, and in the 1960's, Salazar's expressed interest in promoting a truly modern and representative Peruvian theatre had its real beginning. He began to include gay costumbrista touches and his drama, without forfeiting its satirical appeal, approached the humorous. The outstanding creation during this, his third stage of development, is *El fabricante de deudas.*

The final stage of Salazar's career is not clearly discernible, and it can not be proven that he was dissatisfied with the results of his third-stage production. But *El Rabdomante* must be considered unique because none of his other works is similar to it artistically or technically. If Salazar had lived longer, and if *El Rabdomante* were considered a first step towards breaking away from past tradition, it seems reasonable to infer that his future works would have been more universal in their appeal and subject matter, and that the satirical social elements would have been tinged with symbolic and absurd elements as they are in *El Rabdomante.*

The most disturbing feature of Salazar's total dramatic output is the presence of the author's own inconsistencies. Although a number of his works are dramatically, or artistically and technically polished, there are several which are noticeably weak in this respect. A major cause of this phenomenon, which continually plagued him, was the inability to overcome certain structural weaknesses, such as the disparity of the episodic arrangement in several principal works (*Amor, Gran laberinto, Rodil,* and *Algo que quiere morir*). However,

Salazar is to be commended for his overall use of language and his elaboration of dialogues. Whether the language is of a regional or universal appeal, serious or humorous, it is always consistent with the situation at hand.

It does not seem superfluous to assert that, until his death in 1965, Salazar was generally considered Peru's most talented playwright; and that now, twelve years later, no one has been able to challenge or equal his achievements as a dramatist. Salazar's death has proven a blow to the progress of the contemporary Peruvian theatre, and only the passing of time will determine his importance to the recent renaissance of the theatre in Peru.

As one turns from Gibson Parra, Ríos, and Salazar, the recognized patriarchs of Peru's theatre renewal, towards writers of lesser magnitude who also practiced their craft in those early years, the inevitable impression must be that the pages to follow are somehow irrelevant, if not just an exercise in scholarly detail. And it is true that until 1958, the year in which Solari Swayne was internationally acclaimed, there were only a few new and significantly meritorious dramatists to appear on the national stage. In fact, from 1946 to 1958, the theatre in Peru was largely dependent on the developing productions of Ríos and Salazar. This scarcity of experienced and mature dramatists was due essentially to the severe lack of theatrical activity during the late 1930's and 1940's in Peru. Nonetheless, there were a few playwrights who continued to cultivate their art in those lean years and deserve recognition for keeping faith in Peru's ability to overcome, eventually, its past dramatic sterility. From 1946 to 1951, for example, there were two playwrights in particular who gave the added incentive that proved indispensable to the early and formative years of this new theatre. The first of these is José Chioino, who began to create serious drama before 1930, and who continued his efforts through 1950. His works, many of which have a strong costumbrista tendency, are best remembered today for vigorously attacking a variety of social ills that existed in Peru during his life.

Chioino was born in Lima in 1898 and died in 1960. Since 1923, the year of his debut as a dramatist, he made regular contributions to Peru's literary output with his several collections of poems in verse and prose, his newspaper articles, and his drama. Some of Chioino's best known dramatic works are *La divina canción* (1923), *Retorno* (1923), *Una vez en la vida* (1927), *Novio de la emergencia* (1928), *Relato de medianoche* (1940), *La ventana de reja* (n.d.), *La barra rouge* (n.d.), and *El pecado de soñar* (n.d.). *La propia comedia* (1947) and *Tabú* (1950) are the only ones written after 1946. The latter work was awarded the 1950 Premio de la Municipalidad de Lima, but as far as it can be ascertained, the work has never been made available in a printed form. *La propia comedia*, on the other hand, has become one of Chioino's best known dramas and was published shortly after its premiere in 1947.[31]

This work is an adaptation of Tamayo y Baus' famous *Un drama nuevo* (1867), but takes place in a contemporary Latin American setting. It is best

31. José Chioino, *La propia comedia*, ed. Círculo Peruano de Autores (Lima: Empressa Editora Peruana, 1947).

described as a drama within a drama because it is the story of the Dramatist, the principal character in the play, who thinks that his wife is deceiving him and who incorporates a scene into the play he is writing that will allow him to verify the woman's infidelity. *La propia comedia*, just as its model, is unusual in that as the plot develops, the acts take on a double significance because the dramatic situation becomes reality on stage.

For anyone familiar with *Un drama nuevo*, Chioino's indebtedness to Tamayo y Baus is plainly evident. The Peruvian imitates the nineteenth-century Spanish master to such an extent that *La propia comedia* can safely be considered a simple adaptation of the original. Even so, there are several features of the Peruvian work that evidence Chioino's skill as a mature dramatist. The first is his facility with language. The dialogues, for example, progress in a smooth, natural manner and deftly belie any accusation that they are just a reworking of the Spanish original. The characters are also well developed, and even though they are inspired by those of *Un drama nuevo*, they also have a spark of originality that marks them as products of Chioino's own imagination. The Dramatist is the most inspired creation and the Peruvian's portrayal of his emotional instability is truly convincing, particularly in the final scene. Among the secondary characters, the wife of the Dramatist is the most intriguing for the manner in which Chioino skillfully focuses on the emotional crisis she endures as she is drawn between her husband's sentiment and her lover's demands.

There is little doubt that the characterizations and Chioino's use of language in this work best suggest his technical ability and his many years of experience as an accomplished dramatist. But this work is only one of many by Chioino and, therefore, his importance to Peru's theatrical renewal must be understood in terms which are not strictly literary, but psychological. Many of the young writers who met early frustration and disappointment as dramatists have expressed their esteem for Chioino's inspirational endurance and have recognized the incentive his experience has provided. For them it is clear that his success was due largely to his persistence and devotion to a theatre which, at best, was barely alive for so many years.

Bernardo Roca Rey is the second writer who, along with José Chioino, can be considered a major secondary dramatist active during the formative years of the contemporary theatre. Roca Rey was born in Lima in 1918 and attended La Universidad Católica in Lima. By the early 1950's his dramatic production pointed to a future as promising as that of any of his peers. His first play was *Las orejas del alcalde* (1946), a dramatization of Ricardo Palma's *Tradición* of the same title. This work was followed by *Un nuevo pueblo ha de nacer* (1947), a poetic oratory inspired by the Bible; *Loys* (1949); and *Muerte de Atahualpa* (1951). Despite his fair success, however, Roca Rey unfortunately chose not to continue his dramatic production after 1951, the year he terminated his active creation for the theatre. The only feasible explanation for his retirement is that Roca Rey, like Gibson Parra and Chioino, did not fully realize the significance of the early fervor in the national drama and failed to recognize that he, for one, had already made his mark on the newly developing theatre.

Roca Rey's most significant plays are *Muerte de Atahualpa* and *Loys*. The latter, a brief production divided into a prologue and two acts, won the 1949 Concurso de Autores Teatrales Nacionales, and was first staged in 1950 by the Compañía Nacional de Comedias.[32] That same year it won the Premio Nacional de Teatro and was translated into French for its performance in Paris. *Loys* is a brief symbolic drama reminiscent of the traditional auto sacramental, yet it takes place under modern circumstances. The story is a complicated one but essentially concerns Loys, a righteous circus clown, and Niña de la Cuerda, a patent symbol of intellectual reasoning, and their allegorical confrontation with the victorious Satan and his subordinates, greed, pride, corruption, and force. Despite its complications and intrigues, *Loys* is not an enthralling drama, and, from a critical point of view, it is difficult to justify its award-winning status. In fact, this play has proven a perplexing experience for its audiences due to its structural distractions and its insipid use of language. For instance, there is no apparent reason for separating the prologue and the first act, and it is not until the second cuadro of the second act that the author evinces any concern for structural, dramatic, or even thematic unity. In addition, the dialogues are uninspiring, often overextended, and their clarity is often obscured by insignificant symbolic implications. This intentional obscurity, in turn, weakens the characterizations because their individual symbolic roles are not asserted until the closing moments. For all of these reasons, *Loys* is best judged a drama of more historical than artistic significance. Its immediate, although hardly deserved recognition proved only that the aficionados and critics had endured a disappointing year with the national theatre. In a more positive vein, however, the success of *Loys* must have been an encouragement for any dramatist willing to create for a reduced, but loyal public.

Roca Rey's last drama, *Muerte de Atahualpa*,[33] is clearly superior to *Loys* and is unquestionably his best work. It was written in 1951 in Paris, yet it was not presented until 1957, the year it won the Premio Nacional de Teatro. It is based on one of the most popular of the national literary traditions —the circumstances surrounding the death of Atahualpa, the last Inca. Roca Rey's portrayal of the final hours of this popular hero is in one act and begins after the ruler has been captured and has accepted Christian baptism. Atahualpa's plan is that his forces will take advantage of the extra time the ritual affords in order to free him from the Spaniards. But the help does not come and the Inca is dejected by his people's passive resistance. He is joined by Felipillo, the Indian who betrayed him to his enemy, and who has come urging the Inca to admit his inferiority to the Spanish king and thus gain his freedom. As Felipillo listens to the Inca's discourse on the proud heritage of the Empire and why it must stand firm, he realizes that he is still faithful to Atahualpa. But when the traitor de-

32. Bernardo Roca Rey, *Loys*, pp. 6-32, in *Máscara* (Lima: Dirección de Educación Artística y Extensión Cultural, 1950).

33. Bernardo Roca Rey, *Muerte de Atahualpa*, mimeographed (Lima: Asociación de Artistas Aficionados, 1957).

cides to beg forgiveness, it is too late because his leader is being led to his death.

Muerte de Atahualpa was at once a popular creation due to its national identity and dramatic simplicity. More than any of the plays in the 1950's, it had a strong emotional appeal to the Peruvian proud of his national heritage. And by putting particular emphasis on Atahualpa's patriotic defense of his action, Roca Rey makes the work a call for national autonomy and unification and suggests that national greatness can be assured only if there are those who are willing to support Peru resolutely and without regard for personal gain. Even for those (the foreign critics for example) who may have difficulty appreciating the patriotic fervor of *Muerte de Atahualpa*, the play still merits favorable recognition for its substantial technical improvements over *Loys*. The internal structure is of traditional design but cohesive, and as a consequence, the story is developed gradually and in a logical fashion. It does not have the distracting transitional interruptions that plague *Loys*. Atahualpa is appropriately drawn as an imposing figure and his dialogues connote genuine concern for his people and his own exemplary inner strength. Felippillo, although of secondary status, is also impressively portrayed. His ultimate change of heart is especially convincing and substantially reinforces the play's appeal for national unity. *Muerte de Atahualpa* shows particular improvement over *Loys* with regard to Roca Rey's use of language. In his last play he has composed an eloquently refined prose that does much to enhance the dignity of the protagonist. Even Felipillo's dialogue is free of the kind of regional peculiarities and linguistic exaggerations one ordinarily expects in a patriotic drama.

Muerte de Atahualpa, and *Loys* to a limited extent, suggest that Roca Rey's decision to discontinue his dramatic career was an unfortunate one for the national theatre. This is not because these two works are of exceptional quality, but because they show that their author sought to improve his craft and had the artistic potential to become one of the country's better dramatists. With some thematic originality and with continued technical improvement, something which usually comes with experience, it is doubtful that Roca Rey would have remained a secondary dramatist for very long.

THE REALITY OF RENEWAL: PART I

Thus, from 1946 until the late 1950's the renewal of the Peruvian theatre was determined by less than half a dozen writers of recognized merit. And, of these, only Salazar and Ríos were actively engaged as dramatists after 1951. With such a limited number of writers and works, then, it is apparent that this period was especially perilous to the general welfare of the theatre. In fact, there is little doubt that if Ríos and Salazar had not continued their efforts the theatre would have reverted possibly to its previous lethargy and stagnant production, a number of theatre groups would have lost incentive and their faith in national writers, and public enthusiasm would have withered.

In 1958, however, the Peruvian theatre received a vital, if not crucial, inducement to persevere. In that year Enrique Solari Swayne saw the premiere of *Collacocha*, his first drama, and the impact of this work on the Hispanic-American theatre in general was as forceful as that of any work of the decade. For the Peruvian theatre, in particular, Solari's work was a new spark that effectively rekindled the future hopes of the theatre groups, the public, and, significantly, aspiring new playwrights. Within months, Solari was hailed as a new leader of the national stage. His triumph was convincing evidence that the goals and ideals of the renewal of the theatre were within reach and it began the second phase of development, which was to last until the middle of the 1960's. During this period the Peruvian theatre, for the first time in the century, was characterized by an added dimension of dramatic variety and a new-found sense of universal awareness. As new playwrights began to offer their works for public presentation, the national theatre turned even more toward the poetic, individualized, and even experimental dramatic expression, and for the first time since 1946 a common sense of pride and accomplishment was a distinguishing feature of the renewal.

Solari was born in Lima in 1915. He finished his secondary education in the Capital and shortly afterwards, in 1934, traveled to Europe where he lived in Spain and Germany. He began his medical studies at the University of Munich but after three years changed to psychology. In 1947 he returned to Peru where he later became a professor of psychology at the University of San Marcos. The only drama Solari created before 1955, the date of his reknowned drama *Collacocha*, is *Pompas fúnebres* (1954), which is as yet unpublished, and the only works published after that year are *La Mazorca* (1964) and *Ayax Telamonio* (1969).

Collacocha, a three-act drama in prose, was written in 1955 in Huaraz, a small town in the Peruvian Andes.[34] It was first presented three years later in Lima by the Asociación de Artistas Aficionados and within months it was the sensation of the Primer Festival de Teatro Panamericano in Mexico. The following year, in 1959, it was applauded in Bogotá and Madrid. In Chile, it was

34. Enrique Solari Swayne, *Collacocha* (Lima: Populibros peruanos, 1964).

awarded the Premio al mejor autor representado en Chile en 1962 by the Círculo de Criticos de Chile and in Lima it won the Premio Anita Fernandini de Naranjo as the best drama of 1964. Since its debut, *Collacocha* has been presented throughout the world and has been published in numerous editions, anthologies, and school texts.[35]

Before composing *Collacocha*, Solari had spent several years in the Peruvian Andes and, as a result of this experience, became intimately acquainted with the pressing national social, political, and economic problems inherent in this formidable natural barrier. As a reflection of this awareness, his play can be viewed as an expression of his representative concern with Peru's struggle to contain the power of nature in its effort to unite the jungle regions with the rest of the country. Despite its sense of immediacy, however, *Collacocha* affords an optimistic outlook that is based on Solari's faith in his compatriots to win their struggle.

Solari's dramatization centers on Echecopar, an engineer, who is a symbol of faith and determination, and on the tunnel which he is building near Collacocha. In the first act, Echecopar's exaggerated devotion to his task is highlighted with one of his customary patriotic tirades in which he damns the complacency of public officials and all those who put personal interests before the national well-being. He is insanely proud of his accomplishments and particularly of the personal sacrifices he has made during the past eight years of construction.

The second act centers on Echecopar's tragic defeat by the tunnel, which has become a symbol of the power of hostile nature. The first truck driver to use the tunnel informs the engineer that there is a small stream of water at the distant tunnel entrance. Echecopar there discovers that a lagoon on the mountain top above the tunnel is seeping downwards and that the tunnel is threatened with flooding and cave-ins. In an effort to prevent the flooding of lower villages, Echecopar is forced to dynamite the tunnel and a number of workers are unavoidably killed. The third act, which takes place five years later, dwells on the effects of defeat on Echecopar. Fernández has replaced him as chief engineer, but Echecopar still wanders aimlessly about the new tunnel as if he were the builder. Fernandez reveals that his lingering desperation is not due to his defeat by nature, but to the deaths incurred by his decision to destroy the tunnel.

Echecopar enters, and his conversation reveals that, despite his tragedy, he takes pride in those patriots who have carried on the struggle to dominate those natural barriers which have confined so many to misery and poverty. For the second time, the apparently victorious struggle is dramatized by the arrival of the same truck driver who, five years ago, was the first to use the old tunnel. Echecopar is deliriously happy, yet refuses to attend a banquet given by local officials to honor the occasion. Once alone, he hears the voice of a dead worker

35. In addition to the cited ediction, *Collacocha* is included in *Teatro peruano contemporáneo*, ed José Hesse Murga (Madrid: Aguilar, 1963), 319-409; and in *Teatro hispanoamericano. Tres piezas*, ed Frank Dauster (New York: Harcourt, Brace and World, 1965), 183-237.

telling him to rejoice, for the victory may only be temporary because the lagoon is forming again. But Echecopar is not disturbed because he is convinced now that there will always be someone with his kind of determined will to struggle against the relentless hostility of Peru's natural foes.

Thus, *Collacocha* concludes with an optimistic assurance to the national audience. But to champion the work solely on the basis of its regional appeal would be to deny its unquestionable universality rooted in the play's basic conflict, man's ageless struggle to dominate and control nature. So while the regional elements are patently Peruvian, they neither obscure nor restrict the work's appeal to any audience. For instance, the only linguistic peculiarities are the several Quechua words used to announce the arrival of the truck. Otherwise, the language is clear, natural in its development, and unmarred by Peruvianisms. With regard to the dialogues, some critics have pointed to Echecopar's tirades as overly long and declamatory. But they fail to see that to shorten them would weaken the engineer's strong and demanding personality. None of his speeches is a careless arrangement, and each is necessary to the eventual fulfillment of his character. Finally, many of the engineer's comments represent the author's indirect observations on the general political, social, and economic situation he implies as characteristic of Peru and other countries with similar problems. To alter these comments for the sake of brevity would detract considerably from Echecopar's dramatic personality and from *Collacocha's* extraordinary universal and regional relevancy.

The most forceful characterization in this work, that of Echecopar, represents the masses and personifies the common determination that is necessary for national progress. The entire work centers on Echecopar's struggle, and for this reason the destruction of the tunnel in Act II, which coincides with the engineer's personal destruction, is the dramatic climax. The third act serves to reinforce the dramatic continuity. It portrays the effect of defeat on Echecopar and shows that his determined efforts, now alive in Fernández, are finally able to overcome nature's hostility. More emphatically, the third act brings to mind the optimistic message of the play—that even though Echecopar's representative struggle will never be victorious, it will be carried on. Without the third act, Solari's optimistic faith in the Peruvian people would be lost and the basic conflict would lose most of its universal appeal. For these reasons, it is difficult to accept any charge that *Collacocha* is structurally weak and unbalanced. Instead, the last act attests to the author's ability to solve a potentially dangerous structural problem.

La Mazorca,[36] Solari's second three-act drama, was written in Zárate, Peru, and was first presented in Lima in 1965. The action takes place in the present time on La Mazorca, a large plantation in Peru's dense and practically uncivilized jungle. The play portrays the struggle of the García family, part owners of the plantation, against their relentless, often hostile, natural environment. Pancho García, the father, has farmed for so many unproductive years that his

36. Enrique Solari Swayne, *La Mazorca*, mimeographed (Lima: Casa de la Cultura Peruana, 1966).

will to work has been stultified. As a result, Pancho decides to sell his land and return to Lima for a less taxing way of life. Pancho's defeatist attitude ultimately infects the other landowners and prompts them to sell the plantation to a greedy capitalist seeking to establish a land monopoly. In the final moments of the play, the capitalist's ambition is thwarted when the owners admit simultaneously that none of them sincerely wants to abandon La Mazorca and dissolve their friendship. The thematic implication of their collective determination is that they have regained their will to struggle against nature and the faith that they can restrain its onslaught.

While the foregoing summation of *La Mazorca* is not complete, it does point out that Solari's second drama, like *Collacocha*, is inspired in man's contention with his natural environment. Yet there are also some important differences between these two plays. For instance, in *La Mazorca* the hostility of nature does not assume an active role as in *Collacocha*, in which the adversity of nature is constantly referred to and physically dramatized by stage effects at the moment of the tunnel cave-in. In the former drama nature is mentioned as an environmental factor which affects the characters only in an indirect, subconscious manner. The immediate threat to the settlers is inherent in their psychological weaknesses more than in their physical environment. For this reason, the dramatic climax of *La Mazorca* lies in the final decision by the owners to renew and persist in their efforts, and not in any actual struggle against nature, as in *Collacocha*.

A second difference between the two dramas is that *La Mazorca* does not have the powerful social, political, and economic overtones found in *Collacocha*. In fact, Solari includes no direct statements concerning the value of the settlers' contribution to the national effort to colonize and develop the more inaccessible regions of Peru. Neither is there any suggestion of patriotic pride in the owners' unanimous decision not to remain in the jungle. Their decision not to sell the plantation is clearly based on a mutual desire to protect and maintain their friendship, and not on their common interest in the national well-being.

The absence of significant physical action in *La Mazorca* justifies the author's dependence on dialogue to establish and maintain dramatic tension. Unfortunately, a principle weakness of the drama is Solari's failure to create a convincing and natural expression for the characters. Too frequently their dialogue is impaired by declamatory statements and overextension that only strain the audience's sustained interest in the play. Despite these weaknesses, however, the major characters are equally well developed. With the absence of any predominating character, moreover, the settlers may be considered collectively because they ultimately react as a single body and because their faith and determination to continue the struggle against the jungle are bound by a common friendship. In this regard, their collective characterization is reminiscent of that of Echecopar and his successors in *Collacocha*. In both dramas, Solari's message is that the forces of nature can be contended with only if there is a common determination to do so.

In conclusion, *La Mazorca* is a mediocre composition which invites comparison with a superior work by the same author. And due to the numerous thematic and dramatic similarities between the two dramas, there is little doubt that *La Mazorca* is a reworking of *Collacocha.* Even without an awareness of these similarities, however, Solari's second drama suffers from unimaginative characters burdened with uninspired dialogue.

Ayax Telamonio,[37] a long one-act play, is partially inspired in the classical legend of Ajax[38] and in Sophocles' drama, *Ajax.* In Solari's work the action takes place in the present time and on a beach where, after three thousand years, Ayax is still awaiting the decision of his fellow warriors concerning the awarding of Achilles' honorary weapons. Before the decision is reached, six modern youth arrive and are met by the narrator (Relator), who explains Ayax' predicament to them and begs their silence if they stay to observe the outcome. The play action then resumes when Ayax is given the opportunity to defend his right to the arms before the council. Despite his impassioned plea for justice, however, the decision is not in his favor. In order to avenge what he considers an unjust decision, Ayax slaughters a number of animals which, in the night, he mistakes for the council members. After realizing his error, Ayax is even more chagrined and intent on establishing his right to the arms. His final action is to fall on his own sword before the horrified youths. The narrator justifies Ayax' suicide to the youths by stating that it focuses attention on the capricious decision of the council. The narrator's thematic implication is that social injustice, as exemplified by the awarding of the arms, is a constant threat to mankind.

As the foregoing suggests, there are a number of significant differences between *Ayax Telamonio* and Solari's previous dramas. This third work, for example, is devoid of telluric interests, particularly with respect to the struggle between man and nature as dramatized in *Collacocha* and *La Mazorca.* A second difference lies in the absence of regionalisms and references to specific institutions and problems. Solari's criticism is of all men who are unable to discern injustices. These latter departures from Solari's other works, nevertheless, should be viewed in a positive way. They represent his first attempt to break the bonds of regionalism and to appeal directly to a universal audience.

This drama also differs from Solari's other works because his dramatic inspiration can be traced to existing literary sources, particularly the classical legend. *Ayax Telamonio* specifically recalls Sophocles' *Ajax* by its description of the events which take place after the animal slaughter and up to the suicide. Yet, Solari does not imitate the artistic and technical procedures of Sophocles. Par-

37. Enrique Solari Swayne, *Ayax Telamonio,* mimeographed (Lima: Asociación de Artistas Aficionados, 1969).

38. A succinct account of the legend of Ajax is given by Seyffert: "(2) Son of Telamon of Salamis, and halfbrother of Teucer. . . . When Thetis offered the arms and armour of Achilles as a prize for the worthiest, they were adjudged, not to Aias, but to his only competitor Odysseus. . . . Aias thereupon, according to the post-Homeric legend, killed himself in anger. The later legend states that he was driven mad by the sight, mistook the flocks in the camp for his adversaries, and slaughtered them, and on coming to his senses again, felt so mortified that he fell on his sword." Oskar Seyffert, *Dictionary of Classical Antiquities, s.v.* "Aias."

ticularly noticeable are his omission of the classical chorus and several scenes and soliloquies found in the original, the fact that his composition is in prose instead of verse, and his failure to include several of the principle characters of the original *Ajax*. He only mentions Ayax' half brother, Teucer, and makes no reference to his son, Eurysaces. In the classical drama both of these characters are of considerable importance in the psychological development of the protagonist. One of Solari's more effective innovations in the play is the incorporation of the narrator. In this case, the role of the Relator, which is clearly reminiscent of that of the chorus in the classical drama, is to advise the youth as well as the audience of the significance of Ayax' past and present actions. More importantly, his comments and conversation with the youth stimulate the audience's intellectual participation in the drama inasmuch as the youth are no more than dramatic representatives of modern society with which the public can easily identify.

Despite Solari's dependence on well known classical sources and a narrator to aid the audience's comprehension, *Ayax Telamonio* suffers from the author's failure to clarify his thematic intentions. For instance, only after the narrator's explanation in the final moments of the play is Ayax' suicide related to Solari's criticism of man's inability to discern injustice. In fact, without the narrator's final explanation, this play would be a frustrating, meaningless adaption of the original *Ajax*. A second weakness is the distractive and extended presence of the youths on stage. Even though they lend a contemporary note to the drama and elicit the audience's response, their numerous interventions and oral digressions overextend the play and divert attention from the serious nature of the author's criticism.

La Mazorca and *Ayax Telamonio*, then, are not particularly praiseworthy dramas and do not represent Solari's dramatic talents as they are displayed in *Collacocha*. *La Mazorca* is especially disappointing because it is no more than a reworking of the thematic and dramatic formulas of *Collacocha*. Solari's last two plays are significant, nonetheless, because they attest to his continuing efforts as a playwright. *Ayax Telamonio* is the most important in this regard because it indicates that Solari is experimenting with his own dramatic interests and skills. It represents a step towards the kind of thematic and artistic innovations Solari must make if he is to rise above the mediocrity of his last two dramas.

Within less than two years after Solari Swayne had been pushed into the international spotlight by *Collacocha*, Julio Ramón Ribeyro gained extraordinary acclaim in his debut as a dramatist with *Vida y pasión de Santiago el pajarero*.[39] Ribeyro, who has been one of Peru's most popular writers for more than two decades, was born in Lima in 1929 and attended La Universidad Católica de Lima. In 1952, he won a scholarship given by the Instituto de Cultura Hispánica to study in Spain and, before returning home in 1958 studied at the Sorbonne, spent some time in Belgium, and studied in Germany. Follow-

39. Julio Ramón Ribeyro, *Vida y pasión de Santiago el pajarero* (Lima: Universidad Nacional Mayor de San Marcos, 1965).

ing his studies in Europe, Ribeyro spent several years as a professor at the Universidad de Ayacucho before returning to Paris in 1960, where, except for several brief trips to Lima, he has remained.

Ribeyro's works have appeared frequently in various French, Spanish, and German publications and anthologies, and he is recognized principally as the short story writer responsible for introducing a new element into Peru's short narrative, the urban theme. His short story collections include *Cuentos de circunstancias* (1958), *Los gallinazos sin plumas* (1959), *Tres historias sublevantes* (1946), and *Los geniecillos dominicales* (1965). He has also written a novel, *Crónica de San Gabriel* (1960), which won that year's Premio Nacional de Novela; and two dramatic works, *Vida y pasión de Santiago el pajarero*, which won second place in the 1959 competition for the Premio Nacional de Teatro, and a brief one-act farce, *El último cliente* (1966).

Ribeyro's first dramatic creation, which is commonly called *Santiago el pajarero*, premiered in Lima in 1960. It has been such an extraordinary national success that its popularity rivals that of any dramatic work presented in Peru in the past decade. Without a doubt, partial justification of its favorable reception is that it is inspired in one of Ricardo Palma's best known *Tradiciones peruanas*. In this case, the source is "Santiago el Volador," which was originally published in 1875 in the third series of the *Tradiciones*.[40] Both works concern the efforts of Santiago The Birdman to convince Viceroy Amat that man can learn to fly, but Ribeyro's play, which is divided into six brief cuadros, is more than a simple adaptation of Palma's tradición. Even though the former is also set in eighteenth-century Lima and depicts Santiago's plea for aid from the Viceroy, it transcends the historical simplicity of Palma's account to assume a superior ideological conception seated in a satirical attack on twentieth-century Peru's sociopolitical institutions. In addition, Ribeyro has departed from the tradición to add several dramatic dimensions to Santiago's plight. Among these are the fictitious complications to his plans resulting from his love for a woman and from his involvement with several scandalous bohemians. Ribeyro's most important departure from the tradición takes place in the final moments of the play. In order to bring the drama to a climax and to complement its satirical intent, a crowd pushes Santiago off a cliff to mock his ambition to fly and to satisfy their vengeful disposition.

There can be little doubt that Ribeyro wrote *Santiago el pajarero* with a Peruvian audience in mind, yet it is not a play which would be totally meaningless if carried outside of that country's national borders. It is written in a language that is essentially poetic, but not florid, and it preserves the eighteenth-century atmosphere without being awkward or stilted. In short, the dialogues are simple and there are practically no instances in which the work may be said to lag due to the use of language. Structurally, however, there are several questionable elements such as the undue attention put on Santiago's escapades with his bohemian friends and on the final cuadro, which although climactic, is rather insipid in its portrayal of Santiago's death. Nonetheless, the overall divi-

40. Ricardo Palma, *Tradiciones peruanas* (Madrid: Aguilar, 1964), 611-615.

sion into brief cuadros is well executed and justifiable in view of the digressions Ribeyro chose to include.

Ribeyro's originality as a dramatist is best reflected in his character portrayals. Even though they reinforce his indebtedness to Palma, the manner in which he has employed them as satirical barbs of contemporary society is to be commended. To illustrate this point, Santiago can be considered to represent the creative spirit which strives for a better society against such villains as Viceroy Amat, a symbol of inefficiency, irresponsible government, and social inequality. The Professor, who manifests opposition to Santiago's efforts to better himself, represents the kind of intellectual sterility which perpetuates conservative and conformist educational practices. The crowd is a symbol of the wretched social egotist whose goal is to satisfy personal whims, even at the expense of others. Ribeyro has portrayed these, as well as secondary characters in his play, in such a way that, when considered members of a modern society, they reflect his own keen insight into the personal and social weaknesses of the typical cosmopolitan society and of corrupt administrative officials. When considered in the light of its satirical and symbolic characterizations, therefore, *Santiago el pajarero* is clearly a play with a genuine social concern and one which offers a new insight into Ribeyro's characteristic interest in the urban scene.

El último cliente,[41] Ribeyro's second dramatic piece, is a brief one-act farce set in modern Lima and portrays the manner in which an ignominious thief takes advantage of a spinster's emotional weakness in order to rob her. Adelinda, a fifty year-old maid, is closing her clothing rental shop when the Client comes to rent an evening jacket. Instead, he confesses he is a poor lonely man with no use at all for the jacket, and invites the lonely Adelinda to supper. While she changes clothes the Client robs her money box and is about to flee when she returns, anxious to begin her first romantic adventure. Of course her joy is turned to dismay when she discovers the Client slipping out the door to his freedom.

As a farce, *El último cliente* depends heavily upon the variety of emotional responses it elicits from the audience. For example, the initial response is one of pity for each of the lonely characters. Then, when it seems that their friendship is to blossom, the tenderness is suddely replaced by sympathy for Adelinda and scorn for the hardhearted Client. Such emotional changes are to be expected in a farce, but the important point is that Ribeyro executes them in such a brief period of time and in a manner so natural that the characters' puppetlike responses never once distract from the work's realistic atmosphere. The language in *El último cliente* is also in keeping with the realistic overtones of the work since it is of an ordinary conversational quality, simple and direct. It is noteworthy that the aggressive Client's remarks are usually long and declarative, and that the reserved Adelinda generally makes short and straightforward comments. Despite the natural spontaneity of the language, however, their

41. Julio Ramón Ribeyro, *El último cliente*, mimeographed, series 3, no. 6 (Lima: Teatro de la Universidad de San Marcos, 1966).

conversation aptly complements the farcical intent of the work because it is always animated and frequently humourous.

The appearance of Julio Ramón Ribeyro's dramatic pieces could not have surprised those who are acquainted with his artistic versatility, and neither is it surprising that these pieces contain his characteristic urban theme. In keeping with his interests as a writer, his characters are used to reflect Ribeyro's keen insight into the personal and social weaknesses of the typical cosmopolitan and of corrupt administrative officials. In *Santiago el pajarero* particularly their language is direct, yet simple and somewhat poetic without being ornate. The only facet of Ribeyro's plays which can definitely stand improvement is their internal structure, which too often is disorganized and admits digressions. If Ribeyro should write again for the stage, however, it is not likely that he will alter his basically pessimistic view of Peruvian society because, if his short stories and novels are any indication, Ribeyro's drama can be expected to continue his attack on urban ills.

As one reviews the history of the Peruvian theatre renewal from 1946 until the turn of the 1960's, the events occurring during the brief span from 1958 to 1960 seem climactic. In these two years, this theatre gave its best tangible proof that its renewal could indeed become a reality: Salazar Bondy continued to reap laurels with the success of *Dos viejas van por la calle* (1959), Ríos reflected his own departure from tradition with his innovative *Los desesperados* (1960), Solari Swayne presented the national masterpiece of the postwar period, and Ramón Ribeyro inflated popular interest in the drama as few have done in Peru. These individual artistic achievements, when coupled with public participation were also of decisive influence in the formation of the Instituto Nacional de Arte Dramático in 1958, of several private troups such as Grupo Alba in 1960, and even of the Teatro de la Universidad Católica three years later. But perhaps the prime contribution of this fervid activity by established writers, theatre groups, and the populace was its formative influence on those writers who were to come forth as beginning dramatists in the early years of the 1960's. Specifically, there are three dramatists who deserve special mention here because, while they may not be first-rate talents, they proved indispensable to the general progress and stability of the national theatre for the first half of the decade. Their distinctive, at times experimental, dramatic expressions also reflect the renascent sophistication of the national audiences and theatre groups during those years. Neither should it be overlooked that the acceptance of the works of Jiménez Borja, Rivera Saavedra and Elena Portocarrero was extra incentive to the more established playwrights and, especially, to those who were to appear later in the mid-sixties.

The first of these authors, Arturo Jiménez Borja, was born in Tacna in 1908 and was graduated in 1938 from the University of San Marcos as a licensed surgeon. While he has continued his medical career, his reputation with the general public is more solidly based on his published studies on folklore and archeology and, especially, his literary works. He has written several scientifically documented works such as *Iconografía esquizofrénica* (1938), *Taquíes sobre Guamán Poma* (1941), *Instrumentos musicales del Perú* (1951), and *La comida en el antiguo Perú* (1953); several collections of short stories that are based on national legends and include *Cuentos peruanos* (1931), *Moche* (1938), *Leyendas del Perú* (1941), and *Mate peruano*(1948); and three dramatic poems, *Pachacámac* (1958), *La creación del mundo* (1959), and *El hijo del sol* (1964). The latter three works, published under the collective title *Pachacámac*,[42] are brief one-act presentations written entirely in verse and have to do with various aspects of Peru's indigenous myths and legends.

Pachacámac is inspired by the mythical explanation of the great agricultural productivity on Peru's arid coast. According to legend, Pachacámac, the Maker of the Universe, created man and woman, but forgot to provide them with sustenance. After man died, woman pleaded with the Sun for protection and he caused her to give birth to a son who was to be her provider. Pachacámac, however, was jealous of the child and caused his death. The decaying body soon caused a variety of food-producing plants to grow, and since then those who have inhabited Peru's coast have never suffered hunger.

In each of Jiménez' dramatic works, simplicity is the keynote of his presentation. *Pachacámac*, as a representative work, is written in free verse with the predominance of the common eight-syllable line and a vocabulary which reflects a conscious effort to avoid linguistic excess. As a result, the dialogues are more narrative than lyric, and they are usually developed in a succinct yet smooth fashion. *Pachacámac* is also representative of Jiménez' occasional use of characters which are not found in the original myth or legend but are included in order to emphasize the poetic and legendary nature of certain scenes. In this, his first dramatic poem, for instance, he includes characters inspired in indigenous folklore, such as witches, acllas, and mamacuna (the latter two were a kind of matron among the Incas), and even allegorical characters, such as Drought and Solitude.

La creación del mundo is Jiménez' second dramatic poem and one which he describes as a "poema coreográfico." It is simply a series of poetic dialogues in which Night, The Maker, Mother Water, Mother Corn, Mother Cocain, The Condor, The Cat, Man, and Woman tell why they were created and how they can be distinguished from all other elements in the world. This work is the briefest of the author's dramatic pieces, and it is also the least appealing in the dramatic sense. Especially disturbing is the manner in which the intended poetic atmosphere is weakened by the repetitive and narrative nature of the dialogues. Each character introduces himself, and then gives the reason for his creation, often repeating many words that he or a previous character has already used. Such rhetorical and structural repetitiveness in a work as brief as this one is boring and detracts from any dramatic appeal the piece may have.

Jiménez' third and longest dramatic creation, *El hijo del sol*, is inspired in the life of the legendary hero Vichama, who was born from a fragment of the umbilical cord left by the child the Sun engendered in the first woman. This work,

42. Arturo Jiménez Borja, *Pachacámac* (Lima: La Rama Florida, 1965).

then, can be taken as a continuation of *Pachacámac*, the story of the first woman and of the child whose body assured fertile soil on the coast of Peru. According to the legend upon which *El hijo del sol* is based, the young Vichama takes a long and perilous journey across the sea and upon his return discovers that his mother has died. Thereupon the priests bring Vichama her bones, and, after a brief prayer, she is brought back to life. At this point Jiménez departs from legend to invest the work with his own originality. In the final moments of his version, the mother recalls man's turbulent existence and advises Vichama that the only true peace man will find is in death. After she expires for the second time, Vichama is so enchanted by her promise of peace and tranquility that he voluntarily gives up his earthly kingdom to join his mother.

El hijo del sol is the most successful of Jiménez' theatrical productions and the one which best substantiates his reputation as a poetic dramatist. The work also is unique among Jiménez' productions in that, for the first time, he departs from the popular legend to create an original ending. But this addition is skillfully made and gives no indication that the original legend has been changed. Anyone not familiar with the story of Vichama would be unable to detect the author's dramatic alteration because the poetic and legendary continuity is firmly established and maintained from the beginning until the final curtain. Jiménez also includes several characters who have little to do with the basic story and are not included in the legendary account. Their presence, however, is not of an extraneous nature and they dc not detract from the inherent simplicity or the poetic atmosphere of the play.

To conclude, even a cursory evaluation of Jiménez' use of language, of the atmosphere he creates, or even of the characters he portrays, is sufficient to justify the favorable recognition he has received as a poetic dramatist in Peru. And even though his poemas dramáticos have not become box office sensations, they have proven to many skeptics that the poetic drama of simple design can be written in a way that will appeal to the modern audience in Peru. If for no other reason, Jiménez deserves praise for perpetuating a kind of drama that has had limited success in modern Peru.

Among the more sensational of the new dramatists to appear during the early 1960's was Juan Rivera Saavedra. His active career as a dramatist apparently ceased in 1966, but Rivera's production will always attest to the presence of those who, like he, were anxious to present innovative, often controversial plays in Lima. So, although Rivera's works are not artistic or dramatic masterpieces, they have been successful because they have offered Peru's tradition-bound society some original and provocative insights into the problems of modern society. Rivera's interest in the theatre was first manifested in 1959 when he helped found the Teatro Experimental del Ministerio de Educación, a small but active theatre group partially supported by the federal government. In 1961, he represented the theatrical group Histrión at the Seminario de Autores Teatrales in Buenos Aires, and it was during his stay in Argentina that Rivera's creative career began. Since then, he has written several collections of humorous short stories, *Hasta luego tristeza* (n.d.) and *Punto* (n.d.); a novel titled *Loretana* (1965); and his published dramatic works, *1999* (1963), *Los Ruperto* (1965), *Alberto el bueno* (1966), *El gran Tú* (1966), and *Por qué la vaca tiene los ojos tristes* (1966). In addition to his literary pursuits, Rivera is a secondary school teacher and occasionally writes articles of general interest for several daily newspapers in Lima.

Rivera's first two dramas, *1999* and *Los Ruperto*, are dismal creations when judged solely on their artistic merits. Nonetheless, both works were fairly well received by the local audiences because they welcomed Rivera's imaginative presentation of contemporary social topics. *1999*[43] is a challenge to any audience because the viewer must project his thoughts into the future, to the year 1999, when science and industrialization have achieved an incredibly high level of development, when almost all spiritual and moral norms have been lost, and when sentiment and awareness of the soul have been replaced by materialistic desires.

The first act introduces several characters who work for a typical big business in a capitalistic society. They are engaged in the purchase and resale of the human body for organ transplants and research purposes. Certain organs are worth more than others, and the only one which is useless commercially is the brain because there is no place for thinkers in this automated and materialistic society. The second act focuses most of its attention of the firm's price fixing, fear of competition, and the underhanded way it tries to maintain its monopoly in cadavers. In short, it confirms that this is a totally impersonal business concerned only with the material value of the human body. With the explosion and resulting destruction of the warehouse in the third act, the executives finally realize that they have been slaves of a mechanized and materialistic society in which they have existed as mere robots. The play ends as they revel in the rediscovery of their individuality and of the joy of being human beings.

As Rivera's first step to create works of modern appeal and experimental intent, *1999* is an artistic disappointment and is little more than a representative sample of his preoccupation with such pressing social problems as overpopulation, loss of traditional moral norms, and, as seen here, social materialism. It can hardly be considered anything more than an enthusiastic author's first attempt to attract the public's imagination because it proffers no assurance that Rivera is an accomplished dramatist. Structurally, for example, the first and second acts are best described as a chaotic arrangement of extraneous and confusing digressions. This lack of dramatic unity, in combination with the austerity of the dialogues and stereotyped characters, is most distractive when, in the final moments, the audience is left to make its own interpretation of Rivera's thematic intent.

Los Ruperto is a three-act play and was presented in Lima in 1965 by Histrión.[44] It is based on an issue of real concern in the world today, that of

43. Juan Rivera Saavedra, *1999*, mimeographed (Lima: Histrión, 1963).
44. Juan Rivera Saavedra, *Los Ruperto*, mimeographed (Lima: Histrión, 1965).

birth control. The entire work takes place in the home of the prodigious Ruperto family, which is made up of the parents, two grandparents, and fifty-three living sons. The parents, who are seemingly unaware of the miserably crowded conditions in which the family exists, seldom leave their bed because they believe their only purpose is procreation. In the second act the children determine to separate their parents in order to halt their meaningless unions, and their goal is achieved when they lure their father with the promise of a new, mysterious lover. In the third act the father returns after the death of his lover, an anemic old lady, and his future with the family is challenged by several children. Their spirited debate gradually leads to a discussion of the sexual excesses of the parents and, finally, to Rivera's real point in the play, the moral and social implications of birth control. The opposing points of view are represented by a priest and a medical student, recent arrivals on stage. After an overextended debate, the play concludes with no stand being taken by the author.

Los Ruperto, due to its discursive nature and its impact on Catholic Peru, is largely responsible for Rivera's recognition by his cosmopolitan compatriots. But, for the second time, Rivera's popularity is a consequence of his thematic interests, not his talents as a writer. As a result this work does not represent a measurable improvement over *1999* in the artistic sense because the principal weaknesses of the latter are also evident in *Los Ruperto*. In addition to its internal disorganization and numerous extraneous subplots, it seems that the presentation of the principal theme, birth control, could be presented in a manner more impressive than by a closing debate. While the dialogues do show slight improvement, particularly with regard to the transitional passages, they are still somewhat declamatory and riddled with clichés that only stultify any attempt to personalize the different characters. Yet, while none of the characters stands out as an individual creation, it must not be overlooked that the inclusion of so many flat and stereotyped personages reinforces the author's intent to create the kind of impersonal environment that results from overpopulation. This is one of Rivera's principal interests in *Los Ruperto*, and if for no other reason the nondescript characterizations are thematically justifiable.

In 1966, Rivera composed three brief one-act pieces which were presented in a single program and published as *Teatro de humor negro* in 1967[45]: *Alberto el bueno, El Gran Tú,* and *Por qué la vace tiene los ojos tristes.* These works are his best creations in an artistic sense and, through their thematic novelty and farcical nature, drew the attention of numerous aficionados who found that, for Rivera, black humor is a grotesque, ridiculous, and often cruel comment on some facet of human inadequacy. *Alberto el bueno*, for example, is a portrayal of one man's impetuous and imperative kindness. When a neighbor comes to borrow a screwdriver, Alberto cannot find the tool and his frustration turns to violence. When the neighbor turns to leave, Alberto nails him to the door and continues his frantic search for the tool. But Alberto is calmed by his wife and, after the neighbor has gone, Alberto forgets the incident.

45. Juan Rivera Saavedra, *Teatro de humor negro* (Lima: Ediciones Arte Futuro, 1967).

The second work, *El Gran Tú*, dramatizes the cruel and deceitful measures that man will take to satisfy his ego. Gran Tú, a sorcerer who specializes in repairing broken hearts, is approached by a university coed who doubts her sweetheart's love. Gran Tú, however, takes advantage of her innocence and convinces the coed to drink several potions and to subject herself to a masochistic beating. When she is completely drunk, Gran Tú looks to the heavens thanks the sweetheart for causing the coed to visit him, and carries her off to seduce her.

The third work in this series, *Por qué la vaca tiene los ojos tristes*, portrays the horrid effects of extreme jealousy. Miriam has locked her husband, Juan, in a trunk to protect and preserve him for herself. Several characters come to ensure that Juan is healthy and his mother even puts a shawl on the trunk lid to keep him warm. When Miriam hears the sound of kisses emanating from the trunk, she lifts the lid and fires a pistol into the empty trunk to kill the woman who stole her husband's love. It is now apparent that after their marriage, Juan abandoned her for another woman. Since then, Miriam has been insane, and has kept her imaginary Juan in the trunk to keep him safe.

Although there can be no doubt that Rivera's full-length dramas do not substantiate his artistic talents, his brief works are unusually well written and suggest that his withdrawal from the theatre was indeed premature. To illustrate, the internal structural chaos which afflicts *1999* and *Los Ruperto* is conspicuously absent. Rivera demonstrates a sense of careful organization in the manner in which he creates and sustains suspense while subtly teasing the audience's curiousity. The climatic resolution in each work cleverly coincides with the final curtain and, consequently, the audience's involvement is maintained to the maximum. Rivera's use of language is also especially intriguing in his one-act pieces. An interesting and humorous innovation is his frequent inclusion of popular clichés directed in ridicule at other dramatists, perhaps even himself, who commonly resort to such trite devices. Otherwise, as one would expect in farcical works, the language is usually direct and often suggestive, but without being gross. There are few moments in which the dialogue falters, but none in which the characters lose their conversational rhythm or fluency. In conclusion, Rivera's short plays deserve consideration because, in addition to their thematic merits, they substantiate the increasing tendency of Peruvian dramatists of the early 1960's to foment new ideas with the confidence that their public would consider their works as positive manifestations of a maturing, dynamic theatre in search of a new identity.

As it was pointed out in the beginning of this chapter, there were other aspiring dramatists during the 1960's who realized the formative nature of the national theatre and were not reluctant to take advantage of the opportunities it afforded for testing their creative talents. To substantiate this point, it should be noted that as Jiménez came forth with his poetic theatre and Rivera was delving into the possibilities of black humor, the Premio Nacional de Teatro was given for the first time to a female, Elena Portocarrero. But the significant point is that, in addition to being a formal recognition of Portocarrero's first dramatic presentation, *La corcova*, this award proved that deserving works by new writers would be fairly judged, whether by a literary board or the public, and it suggested that their novelty was of significant importance in this regard. This was a comforting reassurance to any new writer who could only envy the success of Ríos, Salazar Bondy, and Solari Swayne. Portocarrero was later joined by other female dramatists, such as Sarina Helfgott and Sara Joffré, and she was even preceded in this regard by several others, such as Delia Colmenares de Fiocco and Carmen de Kun. In addition to *La corcova*, her most important drama, Portocarrero wrote *La espada de madera* (unpublished) in 1961 and *Hoy no, mañana tampoco* in 1966, which was published along with *La corcova* in 1966 in Lima. Both of her published works suggest that, more than any other factor, the italianate commedia dell'arte has been a major influence on Portocarrero's compositions. *La corcova*, for example, which is in verse and prose, is a complicated account of several romantic adventures taking place in seventeenth-century Peru.[46] The first act is a humorous introduction to the characters and suggests the following plot complications. The principle character is Saturino, a servant and confidant who is intent on guaranteeing his master's romance with a certain maiden. The complications in the second act are brought about when a rich widow contracts Saturino to ensure that she and the maiden are pursued by several other men. Saturino, however, takes advantage of his contract to make a financial profit and to protect his master from threatening competition. The third act is entirely devoted to the execution of Saturino's complicated scheme. By an ingenuous use of masks and disguises Saturino skillfully manipulates his clients so that his master wins the maiden, the widow finds another love, and the other characters who have trusted him are financially duped.

Thus it is that *La corcova* while recalling the complicated and intriguing romantic adventures typical of seventeenth-century Spanish theatre is even more reminiscent of the commedia dell'arte. Saturino, for example, is a clear reflection of the famous Arlequin, and the other characters, to an extent, are also imitations of the italianate originals by virtue of their use of masks, their quick wit, and devisive schemes. A second comparison is suggested by the fact that the characters' relationship typifies the usual, yet often impromptu complications that characterize the commedia dell'arte. Instead of reiterating the principle features of this dramatic form as they are found in *La corcova*, however, more attention should be brought to bear on the author's original contributions to the play. One is the intense poetic atmosphere that pervades the entire work and is highlighted by songs such as "La corcova," a modern Peruvian composition, which is the theme song. This work, then, is Peruvian in its setting, characterizations, and song, yet this is not to imply that the regionalistic elements are so strong as to jeopardize its universal appeal.

Structurally, the work is not innovative, but it evidences Portocarrero's strong grasp of the mechanics of the seemingly chaotic and improvisational nature of

46. Elena Portocarrero, *La corcova. Hoy no, mañana tampoco* (Lima: Ediciones Caballo de Troya, 1966), 7-59.

the commedia dell'arte. Even though the initial impression is one of misunderstanding and confusion, for example, the pieces in the romantic puzzle quickly fall into place before the second act is concluded. In the third act the author quickly and decisively ties up all the loose ends. Her talents are displayed equally well by the skillful weaving of extemporaneous, often ludicrously obscure, dialogues. And, true to her inspirational indebtedness, there are frequent moments of comic relief in which the language is racy and even sexually suggestive.

Hoy no, mañana tampoco, Portocarrero's only other published play, is divided into two acts and written in verse and prose.[47] It presents only three characters in its comic situation: an old merchant, who treats his wife with great emotional reserve; the wife, who is anxious to elicit some response from him; and an embobado. They decide on a series of games in which each one, wearing a variety of masks and disguises, tries to intimidate the other. The men's antics soon involve the wife in their flights from reality and together, as each assumes different roles and personalities, their efforts to outdo each other often border on the ridiculous. As the final moment approaches, the husband realizes his past neglect of his wife's emotional needs and she forgets her previous discontentment. The games finally end and the couple's closing song reminds the audience that man can live in loving peace if he can give more of himself and accept more from others.

Hoy no, mañana tampoco, Portocarrero's final composition, was presented in Lima in 1966. Yet even with its farcical novelty, it was not a true success and has not been presented since the year of its debut. One explanation of the work's limited success is its overextension, a result of the excessive number of games, and the several long, sometimes tedious, dialogues that are not in keeping with the truly extemporaneous nature of the traditional commedia dell'arte. It is also true that, in spite of the intriguing use of masks and the improvisational nature of the games, Portocarrero's characterizations here seem rather insipid creations, without the dramatic vitality found in those of her first work.

In conclusion, Elena Portocarrero justly deserves to be remembered, along with Jiménez Borja and Rivera Saavedra, for substantial contributions that, at the time, heavily weighted the balance of the national theatre in favor of sustained growth and meaningful renewal. Although these three writers are not extraordinary dramatic talents, the immediate success of their respective expressions proved that their public and local theatre groups were eager to pursue those horizons which, only years before, were clouded over by tradition and limited opportunities.

47. *Ibid.*, 61-120.

THE REALITY OF RENEWAL: PART II

There can be no doubt that the Peruvian theatre renewal reached an important peak during the period from the debut of *Collacocha* to the mid-sixties. For the stubborn optimist or the patriotic defender, the national theatre was a thriving art form during these years and, by comparison with other national theatres of Hispanic America, was a moderate success. In fact, the optimist's inventory of the theatre's accomplishments was statistically convincing: the number of active national playwrights was greater than at any other time in this century, their total production reflected a variety of interests with a common goal of dramatic excellence, there was an abundance of theatre groups, and popular support for the dramatic arts was steadily increasing. A significant addition to this list is that the national theatre was no longer a substitute term for the Lima theatre. During the early 1960's many authors, theatre groups, and signs of public enthusiasm for the theatre began to appear throughout the country: in Trujillo and Piura on the coast, Arequipa and Cajamarca in the sierra, and even Iquitos in the jungle.

Thus, toward the middle of the decade opportunities for aspiring dramatists were the best ever in Peru. But then, just as quickly as the theatre had begun to prosper in 1958, ominous changes were signalled with the death of Salazar Bondy in July of 1965. His death was indeed a blow because it meant the loss of Peru's outstanding dramatist and an enthusiastic supporter of every facet of the national dramatic ensemble. But Salazar's death was also significant because, with Ríos' withdrawal in 1960 and with the dismal outlook for Solari's production, the Peruvian theatre was left with no active, first-rate dramatist. In deference to the optimistic inventory of months before, it was readily apparent that the recent accomplishments were indeed ephemeral, that the theatre was still in a formative stage, and that renewal was still a goal, not a reality. For the pessimist, the outlook was particularly gloomy. For him, there was no doubt that the future of the national theatre lay principally in the hands of generally inexperienced, even unrecognized, writers and that their works would determine whether twenty years of renewal effort would be wasted due to a lack of national dramatists.

From an historical perspective, therefore, Salazar's death marked the end of the second and gave rise to a third, the present, phase of renewal. In several ways, this latter period has been the most trying—several groups have disbanded, and in some others enthusiasm has ebbed for the want of actors or technical personnel, federal funding for the theatre and for theatre groups has been curtailed, and the pessimistic barbs of some detractors have dampened the spirit of many aficionados and would-be dramatists. In a more positive vein, however, the difficulties of the most recent years have whetted the combative spirit of the truly devoted groups and followers and have aided in determining the innovative spirit and marked individuality of the principle playwrights of this third phase: Julio Ortega, Alonso Alegría, Victor Zavala, and Sara Joffré, all of whom were born after 1935 and, with the exception of Joffré, made their debut as dramatists in 1965 or 1966. Of course, the vitality and progress of the Peruvian theatre since the mid-1960's has not been based solely on youthful innovation and nonconformity. And any refusal to recognize the excellence of the third phase's performance or any dark predictions that a critic may still harbour for the future of this theatre should be enlightened with the understanding of the positive, although different, priorities of the majority of the playwrights and directors in today's Peru. Alegría, Joffré, and Ortega, for example, although they agree with the primary importance of revitalizing the national theatre, have expressed also a preference for a theatre of universal design and appeal. And there is little doubt about their effectiveness in transcending and weakening the enduring popularity proffered by works of a local or regional nature. Even the plays of Zavala, whose *Teatro campesino* is to be identified with the plight of the Andean Indian, have a univeral significance in their exposé of human injustices resulting from social isolation.

A second preference common to most playwrights in Peru today is for a work of unencumbered, if not simple, execution. For these writers, however, the traditionally structured plays with the now trite impositions of suspense and intrigue based on involved plots have given way to a briefer, usually subjective, and, at times, fantastic presentation in which the author's treatment of the story and character developments and the stage sets are most often secondary to his use of language. The logical inference, of course, is that the most recent theatre by Peruvians represents a significant departure from the traditional realistic, particularly the naturalistic, expression. This is not to imply, however, that the two principles of this theatre, brevity and poetic subjectivity, are true innovations in the Peruvian theatre. In fact, the abbreviated dramatic presentation has always been a popular favorite in Peru as well as elsewhere in Hispanic America. Since the past century, for example, brief satirical sketches of local social norms and archetypes, such as those by M. Asencio Segura, have been successful. And with regard to more contemporary precedents of a more subjective, intentionally poetic theatre, one need only recall such dramas as *Esa luna que empieza* (1946), which, although making no radical departure from traditional dramaturgy, does recall the earlier symbolist drama in its treatment of characters, the use of language, and stage sets. It is also appropriate in this regard to remember those postwar writers as Jiménez Borja, Rivera Saavedra, and Salazar Bondy and their brief, one-act plays, which are characteristically subjective and, in some instances, lyric expressions. It is especially noteworthy that Salazar's final play, *El Rabdomante*, is a poetic drama in one act; it stands alone among his historical, realistic, and (by comparison) mundane production and historically is an important milestone in the transition between the second and third phases of the national theatre renewal.

The foregoing has been reiterated at this point to emphasize that, despite their individual preferences and common priorities, those writers to come forth since 1965 have not introduced a totally new dramatic expression. Without wishing to demean the real importance of their contributions or to deny their immediate dramatic heritage, it should be stated that these writers have only developed their drama in a logical fashion—one which is representative of the contemporary and universally accepted norms in the theatre. Nevertheless, it cannot be denied that, for the first time in the history of the Peruvian theatre, brevity, universality, and a poetic sensibility have been combined successfully by a meaningful number of dramatists. As a result, it is obvious that the past renewal efforts were not in vain and that they have not been disregarded. In fact, the third phase writers even have incorporated major elements of their dramatic heritage into a theatre that is evermore a viable entity and ever closer to its goal of a renewed self-identity.

As we turn to those writers who have made their beginning as dramatists since 1965, it would be unjust not to emphasize their youth and to repeat that none was born before 1935. As a consequence, none of these is near the age at which writers are normally considered to be at the peak of their artistic refinement. It is to be understood, therefore, that no discussion of their works, as now known, can be considered complete. Therefore, the following pages provide an introduction to the artists described therein and propose that, based on their proven merits and future promise, the Peruvian theatre now stands at the threshold of its most meaningful achievements since the Second World War.

The most productive of these four writers, Julio Ortega (born 1942) has proven himself in less than ten years to be one of Peru's foremost writers. He began his literary career while a student at La Universidad Católica de Lima. In 1963 and 1964, he won first place in the Juegos Florales of his Alma Mater for his short stories and poetry. In 1964, his first collection of verses, *De este reino*, was published in Lima. Two years later *Tiempo en dos*, a second volume of his verses, appeared with *Las islas blancas*, a book of his short stories. Ortega also is an outstanding literary critic as evidenced by *La contemplación y la fiesta* (1968), a collection of essays on the modern novel, and by his separate studies on José María Eguren, Juan de Arona, and Ventura García Calderón, which have been published in the various editions of *Biblioteca Hombres del Perú.* In 1968 Ortega's first novel, *Mediodía*, was published along with another collection of his poems, *Las viñas de Moro.* He also has been a correspondent for a number of newspapers and magazines, a contributor to recognized literary journals, and a visiting professor at Yale University. At the time of this writing he is residing in Lima.

Ortega was first introduced as a dramatist in 1965. His theatrical debut was made in cooperation with the Teatro de la Universidad Católica in Lima, and consisted of four of his works grouped under the title *Pasos, voces, alguien. . . .* In the same year, the Teatro de la Universidad Católica published Ortega's first collection of drama. The ten works included in this volume, which is titled *Teatro*, are *El intruso*, *La campana*, *Perfecta soledad*, *La ley*, *Se vende cualquier cosa*, *Sociedad anónima*, *Como cruzar una calle*, *El mosto de los lagares*, *Lázaro*, and *Moros en la costa.* Plays written since 1966 are *Aguarde su turno*, *Pedir la palabra*, *La bolsa o la vida*, *Varios rostros del verano*, and *Mesa pelada*, his only political drama. As is so often the case with works by contemporary

Hispanic-American writers, however, those plays not included in *Teatro* are not readily available. Despite several trips to Lima, I have been unable to secure these works, with the exception of *Varios rostros del verano.* Nonetheless, I believe that comment on Ortega's dramatic artistry should not be withheld simply because a few of his works are unpublished or unavailable for analysis. Because his production seems certain to increase, the following observations are offered as a general introduction to his theatre

Since the beginning of his dramatic career, Ortega has been vitally concerned with weakening the traditional interest in Peru in the naturalistic and vaudeville-type theatre. His production is a representative expression of the growing desire in Peru to establish a theatre of modern design that puts emphasis on works with universal appeal, man's problematical existence, and situations with an intellectual basis.

One of Ortega's most intriguing dramatizations in this regard is *El intruso*,[48] a portrayal of *X's* inability to face the fact that The Intruder is gradually replacing him in his work, his home, and his love life. Everywhere X goes he finds The Intruder carrying on his normal activities. *X* never confronts his double, but finally decides to imitate the stranger, in the hope that he might regain control of his own life.

In addition to being Ortega's briefest work, *El intruso* suggests the author's interest in pantomime, inasmuch as The Intruder never speaks and *X's* comments only reiterate what his actions bear out. This, like the majority of the following pieces by Ortega, is inspired in the author's observation of man's reluctance to exert himself for his own improvement. In most of his works a character is presented with a problem concerning his existence, yet takes no action because he is convinced that life is a futile adventure. In fact, man's passive nature before the problems inherent in improving his life is the principal theme throughout Ortega's entire dramatic production.

La campana (Ortega, *Teatro*, pp. 13-21) is similar to the preceding work in that it, too, dramatizes man's passive resistance to forces that work to deprive him of his right to exist. Rov and Vor are imprisoned in a bell and can find no way out. Vor spends each day looking for an exit, but Rov is unconcerned and prefers to pass his time sleeping and eating. Vor finally ceases his search for an exit, thus implying that any effort to free himself from the bell is futile. He confirms his change of attitude in the final moments of the play.

> Es imposible. . . (Silencio) Duerme amigo, sigue durmiendo. Que feliz eres, Rov. Estamos presos, y tú sigues durmiendo. Para ti ni siquiera estamos presos. Yo, yo estoy condenado en una prisión con un hombre que prefiere seguir durmiendo. (*Teatro*, pp. 20-21)

La campana, one of Ortega's most successful compositions,[49] is much more impressive than the preceding work because its dramatic situation is more apt-

48. Julio Ortega, *Teatro* (Lima: Teatro de la Universidad Católica, 1965), 7-11. Subsequent reference in text to this volume will be parenthetically indicated by Ortega, *Teatro*, and respective page numbers.

49. *La campana* has been presented in Lima and in the United States. In addition to its publication in *Teatro* by Ortega, the play also appears in *Teatro breve hispanoamericano contemporáneo*, ed. Carlos Solórzano (Madrid: Aguilar, 1970), 71-76.

ly articulated by action and dialogue, although the latter element is somewhat banal at times. In addition, the theme of the work is clearly manifested in the final moments when Vor finally ceases his search for an exit.

Perfecta soledad (Ortega, *Teatro*, pp. 23-31) has more dramatic substance than *La campana* and *El intruso*, yet it is no longer than either of them. In this work, He begins a conversation with She after asking that they not look at one another and that they not introduce themselves. He contends that any search for true love is futile and that therefore man can only maintain a passive and lonely vigil until the right person happens along:

> Usted y yo no somos el gran amor que esperamos. . . . Esperar, esperar, eso nos hace puros. . . . Confíe. Como yo. Lo encontrará de pronto. Eso es lo perfecto del amor. . . . Nuestra soledad, perfecta ahora, hará que ese amor lo llene todo, que todo lo cumpla. (*Teatro*, p. 30)

She objects at first, but soon changes her mind and agrees that any concerted effort to find the right person is destined to fail. The couple then parts company, with each promising to continue a silent vigil for his true love.

Perfecta soledad is one of the best examples of Ortega's abilities as a dramatist. The characterizations are well drawn, the dialogue is more spontaneous than in many of his other works, and the dramatic situation is intriguing. Even though the play questions man's ability to search out his best mate, there is also a clear implication that man should resort to his reason and patience, not his physiological prowess, in order to find this person.

La ley (Ortega, *Teatro*, pp. 33-42) continues Ortega's characteristic theme of human inanimateness and the absurdity of official institutions by ridiculing the frequently held belief that the perfect state system can really exist. *La ley* presents the story of two policemen in an unnamed state who try to convince a foreign traveler of the flawless nature of their judicial system. It is so perfect, they say, that there are no criminal acts committed, and, as a result, the court system is in danger of decay.

> — Aquí, señor, el sistema jurídico es toda nuestra vida.
> — Hace tanto tiempo que no vemos brillar por su humana eficacia a nuestras leyes perfectas.
> — Imagínese usted que debemos fingir robos para que las leyes funcionen. (*Teatro*, p. 39)

To prevent its complete ruin, the policemen request the traveler to subject himself to a court trial. They promise that he will be found innocent even though he is charged with the most abhorrent crimes. But the traveler, who has never spoken, boards a train and departs. In the hope that someone will agree to help them, the policemen approach another traveler and repeat what they said to the first.

In addition to being Ortega's first work with a satirical intent, *La ley* is different from the preceding pieces in that the peril of man's passive nature is not dramatized by an individual. Instead, Ortega has shown this human weakness by implying that the machinery of the dormant judicial system is rusting due to disuse. In this regard, it should be noted that the policemen's conversation, which is actually a monologue because no effort is made to delineate their separate remarks, is the collective voice of the state's judicial system. Finally, even though *La ley* is slightly longer than the preceding plays, it progresses more smoothly and quickly because of the frequent humorous comments and the spontaneous nature of the policemen's conversation.

Ortega points out the negative values of man's passive nature in some works and in others he dramatizes the tragic results that can be brought about by a zealous and passionate reaction to the problems of human existence. In *Se vende cualquier cosa* (Ortega, *Teatro*, pp. 43-51), for example, he departs from his characteristic theme to show how one man's inability to control his power of reasoning results in murder. A very insolent Salesman has gained entrance to *X's* house, but *X* is determined not to buy any of his trinkets. After a heated argument the Salesman pulls a pistol, *X* reciprocates, and the confrontation seems deadlocked until the Salesman squirts *X* to cool him off. *X* is so shocked that he shoots without noticing that the Salesman's weapon is a water pistol. Then *X* puts the body in his chair, picks up the Salesman's valise, grins, and exits in the victim's original role.

While the theme of *Se vende cualquier cosa* is different from that of the preceding plays, there is little that distinguishes it dramatically. One improvement is the manner in which the dramatic tension is maintained throughout the piece, and this is partially due to the zeal with which the characters defy each other and to the manner in which their demands gradually increase in vehemence. The dramatic climax is reached when *X* shoots the Salesman, and it is at this point that the thematic intent is most clear. Then, when Ortega has *X* assume the Salesman's role, he clearly reinforces his premise that life is an absurd game, yet one which must be continued.

Sociedad anónima (Ortega, *Teatro*, pp. 53-68) returns to Ortega's interest in portraying man's passive resistance by dramatizing the perils of egoism. The sociedad anónima is made up of four sociable, but egotistical, acquaintances whose only common interest is avoiding confrontation with the realities of existence. During one of their meetings, Demetrio, the most unenthusiastic member, arrives with his new sweetheart, Adelaida. She is not impressed with the members' boasting and chides their egocentric evasion of reality. As a result, and despite their dejection and wounded egos, the members accept Adelaida's challenge to overcome their selfish attitudes and to seek a meaning for their existence as Demetrio has done outside of the sociedad.

The play suggests that man must participate actively in life if his personal existence is to be meaningful. Whereas he maintains his animated being by communicating with those around him, he must not permit self-pride to force him into an isolated social position. *Sociedad anónima* is not as dramatically appealing as other works by Ortega because it is overextended, the dialogues are often declamatory and uninspiring, and the denouement takes place too abruptly to be convincing. In addition, one is not aware of the author's thematic intentions until the final moments, and by that time many of the preceding developments seem irrelevant. The play is unquestionably one of Ortega's poorest.

Como cruzar una calle (Ortega, *Teatro*, pp. 69-77) is another of Ortega's short pieces meant to dramatize why man must be aware of those factors which have a direct bearing on his existence. The protagonist is *X*, a man who is unsure of his ability to make a confident decision because he fears the consequence of possible error. In the play, he cannot decide whether to cross a street because he has just seen a man killed by an automobile. This death produces extreme dismay and consternation in *X*, as reflected in the following soliloquy:

> (agitado) Se puede o no se puede volver la vista atrás, ¡esa es la cuestión! No, señor, no. Cruzar o no cruzar, he ahí la alternativa. ¿No cruzar? ¡La calle es el vacío entre dos veredas! . . . (declamatorio) ¡Oh niveles inaccesibles, planos luminosos que así osciláis! (Al centro de la escena) Sobre este vacío la pobre sombra oscilando tan confiada. Ah, si nada más que dos orillas nos midieran. (Empieza a caminar de un extremo a otro, rápido, con las manos cruzadas atrás). Pero, no, las orillas son apenas para las huellas. Claro, uno pone los pies, deja una señal. A pesar del viento. Allí, deja una señal. Pero, y aquí? Aquí la calle es la calle y está vacía. Aquí no quedan huellas. Estamos en el mar, somos el mar y no podemos beber el mar. Y entonces, ¿para qué contarle a nadie ninguna historia? Claro, una historia está en una orilla, es una huella, eso. (*Teatro*, pp. 73-74)

Then *X* queries the woman who has just arrived:

> ¿Es usted capaz de comprender la tremenda, increíble, asombrosa responsabilidad humana, física, invisible, que asume una persona cuando, por propia voluntad, se decide a cruzar una calle? ¿Sabe usted? (*Teatro*, p. 75)

The woman tries to convince *X* that to cross the street is an ordinary event and typical of man's daily actions. *X* is encouraged by the woman and decides to cross the street after a second man arrives safely to the other side. Then *X* closes his eyes, starts for the opposite curb, and is killed by an automobile.

In this work, the author suggests that man should not prolong his existence in doubt and that all decisions must be based on the situation in question. Yet, as suggested by the first of the preceding quotations, the thematic intent of *Como cruzar una calle* is too often obscured or needlessly complicated by *X's* philosophical digressions. Particularly in the beginning moments of the play, the dialogue would be practically unintelligible without the dramatic actions. Only in the closing moments is it clear that *X*, despite being a knowledgeable person, is unable to fulfill the responsibilities of life because he fails to be aware of his immediate environment.

El mosto de los lagares (Ortega, *Teatro*, pp. 76-106) and the following dramas, *Lázaro* and *Moros en la costa*, are considerably longer than the other works in *Teatro*, yet none of these longer compositions departs from Ortega's usual dramatic and thematic tendencies. *El mosto de los lagares* is divided into three cuadros, and is one of the best plays he has written. It presents the story of Juan's return home after an extended absence, and his family's adverse reaction to his presence. From the first moments of his arrival, Juan is aware that his brothers despise him, yet tolerate his return in the hope that their mother's brooding will cease and that the family environment will be more pleasant for them. The brothers, then, resent Juan and blame him for the suffering they have endured during his absence. Once Juan is convinced of his brothers' resentment and realizes that the bond between him and his mother is no longer strong, he leaves home again. But once away he decides to return because he owes a debt to his brothers. Juan's change of attitude is reflected in the following soliloquy:

> ¡Ya es suficiente! Oh, pero qué he hecho . . . Sin saberlo he destruído todo . . . Nunca dije "llevadme al mundo." . . . Pero, soy culpable. Soy culpable desde el primer día . . . Asumo la culpa de mis ojos abiertos. . . Asumo todas las culpas. . . . La primera y la última. . . . La vida partida en padres, en hijos, en pueblos, en hogares que se abandona para siempre. . . . Asumo la espada que nos cortó así, en hombres, mujeres, niños, adultos, vivos, muertos. . . . Yo soy culpable. . . . Debo volver y decirlo. . . . Debo aceptar mi rostro amarillo sobre una pared. . . . Mi rostro entre las sombras, mi silencio de muerto. . . . No debo huir. . . No debo sufrir más. . . . No podría partir sabiendo que ellos, aquí, esperan que yo pague mi condena. Debo cancelar mi sorda deuda. . . . Sí, sí, eso es . . . Ya estaba la vida partida por mitades sangientes, y yo, cruel, terrible, la partí aun más, seccioné todavía con más dolor sus débiles círculos de agua. . . . ¡Yo, yo soy el condenado! Debo volver. (*Teatro*, p. 101)

Juan's compassion, however, is not appreciated, and his brothers murder him for having left the second time. In the closing moments of the play, the irony of his assassination is manifested as the brothers prepare to abandon their home. Now they are convinced that man's destiny is to leave the security of home and to seek some meaning for his existence.

El mosto de los lagares is one of Ortega's most accomplished dramatic works, and is also the most elaborate expression of his pessimistic outlook for mankind. My only criticism is that the basic simplicity of the plot and its development are sometimes complicated by Juan's long and bewildering soliloquies. These weaknesses are found frequently in Ortega's theatre, but they are even more apparent in his longer works. Nonetheless, those who are able to follow Juan's cerebral digressions will discover that man is doomed to a tragic end because he cannot bear passive resistance to his problem and because his brotherly compassion is also an unacceptable solution.

Lázaro (Ortega, *Teatro*, pp. 107-139) is also divided into three cuadros and is Ortega's only dramatic piece in verse. It is an indictment of man's worldly existence, yet it includes no specific reference to man's passive or passionate nature. Instead, *Lázaro* is intended only to dramatize the anguish and futility of worldly existence. The story is inspired by the Biblical account of Lazarus' resurrection, and takes place after he has returned from the dead. In Ortega's adaptation, Lázaro is not happy with his new life because it means nothing to him. Throughout the work Lázaro ponders the anguish and the insignificance of his existence.

> Si a la noche responde otra noche
> y del hueso del mundo monda la muerte
> con diente ávido, o somos cada uno
> también gusanos de la tierra
> y es la tierra fea tumba
> y mordemos un cadaver maloliente. . .
> O trae la noche otra sombra, otra agua,
> y apenas si dormidos del sueño un hilo

nos cose a la vida, o la vida
nos desteje en los días, o somos
una pobre madeja, sucia lana,
y todo esto, ¿para qué? (*Teatro*, pp. 133-134)

In a desperate search for some meaning for his life, he arrives in Jerusalem just before Christ is to be crucified and at the time when the peoples' malice and derision are at their height. Then after the thunder and lightning that mark Christ's death, the masses become fearful and implore divine forgiveness. Lázaro chooses this opportunity to belittle their fear and to ridicule their remorse.

¡Alto! ¡Alto! ¡Deteneos temblorosos
asesinos! ¡Que! ¿Gemís acaso
o contemplo una marcha de pálidos
gusanos? ¡Ya sois libres!
¡Ya tenéis las manos rojas!
¡Qué feliz gente! ¡Bailad, bailad
de contento! . . .
¡Tembláis como ladronzuelos!
Sois libres, sabedlo. ¡Habéis
ganado con sangre vuestra sucia libertad!
¿Habrá entre vosotros un hombre
que vista con el silencio
y no con tibio llanto?
¿Ha muerto para que tembláis? (*Teatro*, p. 137)

His mockery so enrages the people that they kill him, but Lázaro dies laughing because he knows that his assassins are only delivering him from the anguish and futility of human existence.

Lázaro is a pessimistic play devoid of intentional Christian doctrine. Lázaro does not rejoice in death because of his religious devotion, but because he knows that death is preferable to life on earth. Yet, while this work suggests an interesting interpretation for the original story of Lazarus, it is disappointing with regard to the use of language. Even though the play is written in free verse, the dialogues lose much of their intended linguistic appeal because they are more narrative and prosaic than poetic. The drama also exemplifies Ortega's tendency to obscure the thematic simplicity of his creation with needlessly complicated ideological and philosophical inferences. As one plods through some of the dialogues and endures constant reiteration of Lázaro's plight, it becomes clear that Ortega might have developed this play with less emphasis on the intellectual and more on its thematic clarity. This is particularly true inasmuch as *Lázaro* has more dramatic potential than many of his other works.

Moros en la costa[50] (Ortega, *Teatro*, pp. 141-164) takes place in a library which displays the statues of Don Quijote and Sancho Panza, Don Juan and Doña Inés, Hamlet and Ophelia, Faust and Margarite, and Mephistopheles. Each night the statues become living creatures and descend from their pedes-

50. "Hay moros en la costa" is a traditional saying that was used to warn against an impending Moorish invasion of the Iberian Peninsula.

tals to play canasta. With the exception of Mephistopheles, all of them are now decadent human beings, as suggested by their constant concern with petty matters and by their mutual envy of the cautious Mephistopheles. They realize that he is the only one among them who has preserved his original fame and personality, and they resent his presence. In the closing moments of the play, when they are no longer able to tolerate Mephistopheles' critical suggestions, they attack him. But he escapes certain death because they have to return to their pedestals the moment their wrath is vented. The play ends as Mephistopheles, hobbling to his pedestal, laments his inability to warn his companions of further degradation.

Moros en la costa, the last work included in the published volume of Ortega's dramatic pieces, is a return to his characteristic theme, that of man's passive nature. It is a rather simple play dramatically, and the thematic involvement is equally uncomplicated. The drama has a special imaginative appeal and admirably reflects Ortega's artistic originality in the way he gives a "behind the scene" account of the once famous characters' new lives. Their dialogue is well written and the attempt to personalize each one's manner of speech is strikingly inventive.

Varios rostros del verano,[51] which in its original version was titled *Noches extrañamente divertidas*, was awarded second place in the 1968 Concurso Nacional de Obras de un Acto. That same year, it was first performed by the Teatro de la Universidad de San Marcos. This play also is an integral part of Ortega's only novel, *Mediodía*. Although this work does not differ thematically from Ortega's other dramatic pieces discussed herein, it is more involved than they in that the author's characteristic theme is supplemented with a number of related philosophical tenets, all of which are found in his other dramas. In this as well as in certain other works, Ortega dramatizes man's absurd concern with the trivial aspects of his condition, the egocentric defense of his hermetic existence, and the irony of his pessimistic outlook. *Varios rostros del verano*, then, is a synthesis of Ortega's philosophical postulates as expressed in his entire dramatic production.

Mur and Nin have been meeting regularly in a bar during the summer months. Each time their discussion has been based on a mutual preoccupation with death, and the doubts and uncertainties concerning life after death have made their existence an agony. One night Mur enters into a dream state that is progressively reinforced by the alcohol he is consuming. During an ensuing conversation, Nin functions as Mur's conscience. Even though Mur is never able to ascertain Nin's true identity, it is apparent that Nin's different roles represent the memory of those beings with whom Mur has had some relation: his father, a friend, God, the Devil. As Mur answers Nin's questions, he relates a number of his vital experiences, all of which point to his characteristic withdrawal from those personal relationships which could lessen or even terminate

51. Julio Ortega, *Varios rostros del verano*, mimeographed (Lima: Teatro de la Universidad Católica, 1968). This copy of *Varios rostros del verano* was prepared for the play's premiere in Lima on 10 February 1968.

the agony of his solitary existence. More importantly, Mur's answers reveal that whether he is aware of his conscious reality or lost in subconscious meditation, he is unable to escape his preoccupation with death and the thought that he has begun to die. This point is evidenced by Mur's admission before returning to conscious reality that he already feels dead:

NIN: Ha llegado tu hora, muchacho. Prepárate. . . . Confiesa que quisieras huir de este lugar. Confiesa que aquí se vive muriendo a chorros. . . . ¿Ya has muerto?
MUR: Creo que ya.

The work ends with the characters' repeating their opening statements—that they spend each evening, regardless of the role each might play, attempting to escape their conscious reality because they do not want to continue to suffer their thoughts of dying.

MUR: (A la platea) Así señores y señoras, todas las noches muere uno de nosotros. Esta vez me ha tocado a mí.
NIN: (A la platea) Es la historia de dos viejos amigos que . . . no quieren seguir muriendo. Es su manera de evitarlo. Todos tienen su manera de evitarlo.

Of course the tragic irony of their own deceit is what makes the lasting impression upon the audience.

Julio Ortega has indicated a fondness for *Varios rostros del verano*, along with *La ley* and *La campana*.[52] The play has been reworked on at least three occasions and as a result is Ortega's most carefully elaborated drama. Structurally, for example, the play-within-a-play arrangement clearly focuses one's attention on the subconscious state of Mur and lends double significance to the dramatization of the basic theme of man's passive attitude towards his problematical existence. In addition, the close relation between the structure and the theme is substantiated by the harmonious balance maintained between the language and the action. Although the play is essentially dependent on dialogue, the physical roles of both personages, particularly of Nin as he assumes the different identities, are an integral part of the character delineations and a welcome complement to the audience's interpretation of the theme of the play.

It does not seem an exaggeration to assert that *Varios rostros del verano* is Ortega's best drama. The dialogue is free of extraneous interventions and digressions, which, as in several other works, tend to weaken and obscure the thematic unity. The author has also taken care to avoid possible confusion resulting from abrupt transitions from one thought process to another. Also, each character's psychological identity is maintained during the dream sequence. This is an important factor inasmuch as Nin and Mur, like Rov and Vor in *La campana*, characterize separate aspects of man's existence. Mur is the voice of conscious awareness, and Nin is the voice of subconscious being.

Mesa pelada[53] is Ortega's single work of historical inspiration and his most recent to be presented in Lima. It was composed in June 1969 in Mexico and, in

52. In response to my expressed interest in these three plays, Ortega wrote: "Me complace mucho que Usted haya pensado precisamente en las tres piezas mías que más quiero, que mejor fortuna tuvieron." Julio Ortega, Lima, Peru, to Robert J. Morris, Lubbock, Texas, 28 September 1971, *in* Texas Tech University Library, Lubbock.

53. Julio Ortega, *Mesa pelada, Textual, Revista de Artes y Letras*, 2(septiembre 1971):20-29.

1971, received the Premio Nacional de Teatro para Obras de Corto Reparto, the new designation for the Premio Nacional de Obras de Un Acto y Monólogos instituted in 1966. This one-act play consists of four ensayos, or versions, of the death of Luis de la Puente Uceda, a young rebel, at Mesa Pelada, Peru in the early years of the past decade. One version is that of de la Puente's supposed uncle, and the three remaining versions are those of soldiers who participated in the capture that lead to the rebel's death. But as Ortega is quick to point out in the notes which accompany the edition cited, and as the work itself aptly substantiates, *Mesa pelada* bears no political preferences and is not intended to martyrize either de la Puente or his revolutionary aspirations. The real purpose of the play is to dramatize its author's abiding concern with the horrors of armed conflict. The tragedies of the rebel and the soldiers are intended only as representative consequences of such a struggle and persecution. On a third level of interpretation, *Mesa pelada* represents an attempt by each of the individuals involved to understand de la Puente's suffering and to justify the agony resulting from the participation of each of these individuals in this event, which, for Ortega, is typical of the inevitable tragedy of armed confrontation.

However, despite the unique source of inspiration for *Mesa pelada*, it is still characteristic of Ortega's portrayal of man's inability to avoid the consequences of his own acts and decisions. From a technical point of view, the play is not typical of Ortega's theatrical works written before 1968 because it substantiates, along with *Varios rostros del verano*, the contention that since the late 1960's, at least, Ortega has been increasingly concerned with improving the artistic aspect of his drama. Particularly appealing in this work, for example, is the manner in which Ortega has sought to assure a spontaneous continuum from one ensayo to another with the use of only four actors, A1, A2, A3, and A4. These actors, who never abandon the stage, have no special identity except when they temporarily assume any one of the several character roles. Otherwise, they are anonymous secondary characters, or voces who question or briefly comment on the version being related. As a result of the technical flexibility inherent in such a basic dramatic deployment of the actors, then, Ortega ensures that the transition from one ensayo to the next is always a simple and non-disruptive execution—there being only a slight pause and no scenery to change or new actors or characters to introduce to the stage. In the final moments of the play, there is a brief epilogue in which the four actors, and in a manner reminiscent of the classical chorus, successively reiterate the real tragedy of the death of de la Puente: that even the tragedy itself has been forgotten having left no legacy.

Several conclusions about Ortega's drama can be drawn from the preceding observations. The most apparent is that all of his pieces are relatively brief and simple. Brevity and technical simplicity are indispensable complements to Ortega's effort to dramatize his philosophical concerns in a logical and efficient manner. Nevertheless, some of his works suffer from technical weaknesses that adversely affect their thematic clarity. In his longer works, for example, extraneous or repetitive dialogues frequently appear, often in the author's attempts to strengthen the philosophical fiber of his play or to add a note of intellectual profundity. Too often these dialogues are declamatory and overly prosaic, even in *Lázaro*, his only drama in verse. As a result, many of Ortega's dialogues are distractive additions and fail to become an integral part of the dramatic whole. However, in those works having only a few pages, such as *La ley*, *La campana*, and *El intruso*, the dialogues have no serious defects. They are concise, usually spontaneous, and have sequence.

Ortega's character portrayals are somewhat unimaginative, as is his use of language. Too often it is obvious that the characters are verbal devices that have been created only to express the author's philosophical evaluation of man's existence. And because Ortega's usual philosophic intent is to reflect man's characteristic passivity, he has not seen fit to invest his personages with distinguishing character traits. Consequently, there are practically no artistic or psychological variations between the principal characters in each of his works. In fact, Ortega's characters are usually dehumanized creations devoid of authentic human appeal or interests such as love, sex, or a sense of humor. There is no strong or impressive character, nor is there one with a sense of originality that might free him from being a simple representative of man in general. Ortega's most interesting characters, from a dramatic point of view, are found in *La campana* and *Varios rostros del verano*. In these works the characters can be considered to represent different facets of one man's being. In the former play, for example, Rov and Vor are reverse images of one non-existent personage. Nevertheless, they are still symbols of man's passive and passionate nature and, as such, are not to be construed as a variation of Ortega's typical character portrayals.

Like a great number of present day European and North American dramatists, and even the ancient Greeks, Ortega is preoccupied with the ordinary problems of man's existence. Throughout his production, he implies a concern with man's inability to evolve some plan by which he can adequately cope with the consequences of daily living. Thus, Ortega's principal theme is man's ineffectiveness when dealing with even the ordinary problems of his existence. For Ortega, whether man is a passive or passionate being, he characteristically fails to heed the reality of his situation and makes unwise decisions, which only aggravate his miserable situation. Other of Ortega's underlying interests, although they are not mentioned directly in any of his plays, are man's inability to communicate effectively and the manner in which his egoism helps isolate him from society. Essentially, then, Ortega's drama dwells on man's incapacity to surmount obstacles and on the futility of his efforts to improve his existence. His entire dramatic production is an ironic statement that life is an absurd experience that must continue, and that any reaction to one's existence is also absurd.

The theatre of Julio Ortega has been a valuable addition to Peru's increasingly varied and cosmopolitan dramatic offering. And among that nation's young dramatists, those who have begun to write for the stage since the early 1960's, Ortega has made the most decisive steps towards severing Peru's unusually strong bonds of tradition and establishing a theatre of universal appeal. Careful scrutiny reveals, however, that its success is due more to Ortega's philosophical and thematic tenets than to its dramatic and artistic merits. As a consequence, his plays often seem unpolished dramatizations of his own philosophical postulates. It is apparent that Julio Ortega has just begun his career as a dramatist, and additional experience and artistic maturity should allow full realization of his capacities.

Within the total scope of activities that comprise the dramatic arts in present-day Peru, there is no one more involved than Alonso Alegría. But this is not to imply that he is among the country's most productive dramatists. In fact, Alegría's reputation is not based solely on his dramatic compositions, of which only two have been completed and staged. Besides those works, and at least one other drama in progress, Alegría has exercised considerable talent as a director, producer, and theatrical entrepreneur for more than a decade, having been active in such roles during his early twenties.

Alegría was born in 1940, in Santiago, Chile, but received his primary and secondary education in Lima. By the late 1950's, as he began his university studies, he was already a serious devotee of theatrical arts. It was in 1960, during his third year of architectural studies at the Catholic University in Lima, that Alegría finally determined to pursue a professional career in the theatre, and to do so on a full-time basis. This was not a radical or unexpected change; for more than a year, he had been collaborating with the internationally acclaimed director Reynaldo D'Amore in Lima's Club de Teatro and with the Teatro de la Universidad de San Marcos. In 1960, he also founded Grupo Alba, an independent troupe, and directed several of its plays. One of these was his own adaptation of Saroyan's *The Beautiful People.* In addition to these experiences and to his own expertise, a major boost to Alegría's career development came in the early 1960's when he received a Fulbright Scholarship to Yale University. There he finished a baccalaureate in 1964 and, two years later, a Master of Fine Arts degree. Since then Alegría has worked professionally, producing and directing more than thirty plays with such institutions as the Yale Repertory Theatre, the New York Shakespeare Festival, and with numerous groups in Lima. Since 1971, he has been the director of the Teatro Nacional Popular in Peru. This is a federally funded organization under the auspices of the Instituto Nacional (which replaced its predecessor, the Case de Cultura Peruana, in 1971). The Teatro Nacional Popular (T.N.P.), as stated in its charge from the national government, is expected to promote every aspect of the dramatic arts throughout the country, especially at the grassroots level. After assuming the directorship of the T.N.P., Alegría pointed out that he did not intend to elaborate a plastic, absurd, or conceptual drama. His goal, in keeping with the design of the organization, is to foment the theatre as a viable form of communication among the various segments of the populace. Obviously, its appeal will not be to the elitist or to the aesthete for whom artistic purity is a refuge from reality.

For the skeptic, this may appear a futile, if not undesirable, assignment for one of Alegría's preparation and artistic temperament. And Alegría has admitted that he has yet to find material which he deems suitable or which conforms to the goals of the T.N.P.. With respect to this problem, he has commented:

> Esa es la gran búsqueda, eso es lo terrible, que no exista material escrito que se adecúe plenamente a los intereses del grupo. . . . Tiene que haber un proceso de elaboración, de adaptación, de reescritura, un proceso de decantación de gente para que se escriba para el teatro de acuerdo a este nuevo lineamiento.[54]

The purpose for delving into the scheme of the T.N.P. is twofold. First, I would point out that it represents one way in which the contemporary Peruvian theatre is actively seeking change and improvement and, in this instance, with government approval and support. No other group in Latin America is similar in its constitution and charge. Second, discussion of the T.N.P. is essential in order to emphasize the active and multifaceted involvement of Alegría in the national theatre—to show that even though the T.N.P. has not yet fulfilled its charge, it is not because Alegría, the entrepreneur, has failed to rally public, private, and even additional government support for this organization. He, more forcibly than any individual in Lima today, has contended that the future of the national theatre should be reckoned with now, that the outlook is optimistic, and that Peru needs to cultivate her own talents at every social and cultural level. His strong voice has been an invaluable stimulus to every sector of the theatre, from the elitist to the grassroots.

As we turn to Alegría's dramas, it should be reiterated that he did not begin his career as a playwright and that, while his works undoubtedly account for much of his renown, he has always devoted the majority of his efforts to directing and producing. This is not to derogate Alegría's production. To the contrary, it is to assert that, due to the demands on his several interests as a theatrical artist, Alegría has developed his literary talents in an irregular fashion. He is, of course, aware of the seemingly disparate division of his interests and, in 1971, offered the following observations on this aspect of his career:

> No pensaba . . . seguir dramaturgia, pero me dieron una beca para dramaturgia y en el fondo todo el mundo quiere ser escritor. Es decir, en el teatro, la más efimera de las artes, quien no quisiera dejar puestas en una página unas ideas que perduren más allá de la última función. Y poco a poco me ha ido gustando más y más escribir, hasta que ahora llego a considerarme tanto dramaturgo como director. Me he preguntado qué es lo que prefiero y no sé responder. Me he podido pasar sin escribir dos años, pero cuando dejo de dirigir extraño los ensayos, el trabajo, las funciones.[55]

Alegría's first drama, *Remigio el huaquero*, premiered in Lima in 1965 and shared the Premio Nacional de Teatro with *El Rabdomante*, the last work by Sebastián Salazar Bondy. *Remigio el huaquero* (huaquero being a word derived from the Quechua huaco, almost any type of ceramic vessel) brings pressure to bear on an insistent foe of the Peruvian government in its struggle to preserve intact the national pre-Conquest treasures. A huaquero is one who illegally hunts, digs up, and disposes of the ancient relics, artifacts, and other such valuables left to modern man by the pre-Inca and Inca empires. The huaquero is

54. Bruno Podestá A., interview with Alonso Alegría, "Teatro Nacional: Un teatro popular o la popularización del teatro?" *Latin American Theatre Review*, 7 (Fall 1973):33-41.

55. Alonso Alegría, "El teatro es una infección," *Textual, Revista de Artes y Letras*, 2(septiembre 1971):4.

often an uneducated individual who, in turn, is exploited by a clever swindler who secretly sells the treasures to private collectors. Alegría's drama, one of few Peruvian works to admit the continued existence of such individuals, is more than just a vivid portrayal of personal greed; it is a comment on social graft and corruption.

Each of the three acts is divided into two lengthy scenes; five of the six scenes are laid on the arid coast of Peru near the pre-Inca ruins of Chancay. For years Remigio has searched these ruins for a fabled buried palace and its treasures, but it is Juan, his son, who accidentally uncovers a valuable golden vase. Enrique, a friend who illegally traffics in such treasures, subsequently appears to appraise the relic. Realizing his opportunity for considerable profit, he deceives Remigio and pays him only a pittance for the vase. The first act then ends with the news that Juan has been stricken with the mysterious disease which killed his mother long before.

In the second act Remigio is convinced by a curandero, also a friend, that the vase must be recovered if Juan is to be cured. In his ensuing search for the vase, Remigio ultimately discovers that he was deceived by Enrique, and that the latter, in turn, has been deceived by Gunter, a wealthy dealer in national treasures. The final act dramatizes the end of Remigio's career as a huaquero and his realization of the pernicious effects of wealth upon the greedy. When he returns home with the vase he finds that Juan's sickness was not serious and that even the curandero had lied with the hope of possessing the vessel for himself. When Remigio is alone and burying the vase, he speaks of the evil way in which men and friendships can be destroyed by greed. Moreover, convinced that his belief in the buried palace is only another deceit and a result of his own greed, he decides to search no more for its treasure. So great is Remigio's fear of wealth now, that he will not even sell the vase so his son may go to school.

There can be little doubt that Alegría's initial dramatic piece is intended for the local audience more than for any other. In addition to the place names, the implied criticism of those who destroy the national treasures and even the types of characters in the play are commonplace to most Peruvians. If it were presented to any other than an Andean public, *Remigio el huaquero* would certainly forfeit much of its popular appeal and thematic impact. Its most universal aspect, after all, is the implication that the love of money is the root of all evil, and this point is stressed only in the final scene.

The characters are, on the whole, stereotyped individuals who represent some of the most common types of Peruvian society: Juan is the youth whose education is to suffer from another's avarice; the curandero and Enrique represent the individual who thrives on the ignorance, gullibility, and superstitions of the masses; Gunter is one of the social elite that thrives and protects himself with wealth and political influence; and Remigio, the pathetic individual who knowingly lives outside the law in his struggle to survive and is the logical victim of the greed of others. But because types such as those just described can be found in most societies, Alegría has reinforced the regionalistic appeal of the play by placing them within a representative stratification of Peruvian society, one based on racial and economic criteria: Juan and Remigio are pure Indians and, as such, are poor; the curandero, a mestizo, is barely more affluent than the huaquero and his son; Enrique, also a mestizo, is the middle-class Peruvian of limited monetary capabilities struggling to survive in an increasingly commercialized society; and Gunter is the rich white merchant and member of the upper social strata. On the basis of such stereotypes, then, *Remigio el huaquero* can be construed as a weak protest of Peruvian society and an indirect statement that the country's class barriers, in particular, are a result of its own economic and social norms and priorities.

Despite its national recognition in 1965, *Remigio el huaquero* has not been made readily available to the public. This presentation, for instance, is based on Alegría's own translation into English entitled *The Buried Palace*.[56] Due to the unavailability of a Spanish version, and because there are numerous errors in the English translation, a fair evaluation of Alegría's use of language is not possible. But some mention should be made of the fact that, even in the English version, the dialogues reflect considerable care in their presentation of ideas and exchanges and contain no objectionable extraneous elements. The play's greatest technical weakness is its length; the first act, particularly, would be measurably improved if it were shortened. It is more than twice as long as the third act, and half again as long as the second. Otherwise, Alegría's first drama is to be commended for its structural balance and continuity, which is due, in part, to having followed traditional and conservative techniques and norms in its composition. He has adhered closely to the three unities, the play's satirical elements are subdued and general in nature, and, in a fashion reminiscent of nineteenth-century drama, the moralizing didactic is reserved for the end of the play. Despite the obvious dependence on proven formulas of the past, however, Alegría's work is a refreshing, perhaps nostalgic portrayal of a segment of Peruvian society which has escaped dramatization for a number of years.

Alegría's second drama is remarkably different from his first. When viewed along with his other activities in the national theatre, it is the mainstay of his reputation as a major innovator of this theatre. *El cruce sobre el Niágara*[57] was composed in 1968, the year it won the Premio Nacional de Teatro para obras en un acto, and in 1969 it was presented in Lima by the Teatro de la Universidad de San Marcos and received the drama award offered by Casa de las Américas in Cuba. Since then, the play has been presented by numerous theatre groups throughout the Americas and, more recently, a recorded version has been made available for educational purposes.[58] Consisting of six scenes and a prologue, *El cruce* is based on the historical exploits of Jean François Gravelet (1824-1897), a French tightrope walker and acrobat known profession-

56. Alonso Alegría, *The Buried Palace*, trans. Alonso Alegría, typescript, 1964, Texas Tech University Library, Lubbock.

57. Alonso Alegría, *El cruce sobre el Niágara*, mimeographed (Lima: Teatro de la Universidad de San Marcos, 1969). Subsequent reference to this text will be indicated parenthetically by *El cruce* and appropriate page number.

58. A printed copy and a tape recording of *El cruce sobre el Niágara* was first offered for sale in 1971 by The Center of Curriculum Development, Inc., 401 Walnut St., Philadelphia, Pennsylvania.

ally as Blondín. In Alegría's drama, Blondín is portrayed as a realist, somewhat pessimistic, and egocentric. The second character, the younger Carlo, is a contrasting figure because he is more idealistic, overly optimistic, and frustrated by a sense of cowardice. Despite their apparent differences, it is soon evident that Blondín and Carlo have a marked likeness psychologically because each is living in an existential void and is looking for a way to recover his vital essence. Blondín admits that he no longer has pride in his performance, and Carlo confesses his need to prove his valor.

Carlo first approaches Blondín to accuse him of fraudulent practices, namely of preparing and eating an eight-egg omelette, rather than the twelve-egg version promised, while on a tightwire over Niagara Falls. After several such encounters with Carlo, and in order to dispel other rumors of sensationalism and deceptive practices, Blondín accepts the challenge to cross Niagara Falls with his antagonist on his back. Carlo has convinced Blondín that a successful performance would give him a new sense of self-fulfillment and relieve his vital anguish. Carlo is also anxious to make the crossing in order to regain his pride and put an end to his own source of frustration. After weeks of preparation, the two men reach such a state of coordination that they accomplish the feat as if, mentally and physically, they were one being. This state of perfection they call Icarón. In addition to the sobering reminder that his Icarón, as was his Greek model, is subject to death below, Alegría is also implying that the swirling waters below Niagara represent the vital abyss from which his Icarón (Carlo and Blondín) has symbolically ascended. Moreover, their determination and ultimate success constitute Alegría's thematic implication that man must not abandon his struggle for self-fulfillment; if he does, he is sure to suffer the throes of his own existence.

Alegría's masterful elaboration and coordination of the dramatic structure and thematic message is most discernible in the closing moments of the drama. It is then, after the long and careful training and preparation which lead to the creation of Icarón, that the climax of the action, the crossing, is reached and the thematic intent is manifested. Only then does each of the characters realize his most satisfying moment of personal fulfillment. Blondín discovers that his acceptance and subsequent dependence on Carlo has afforded him his most difficult triumph, the one which before was only a dream. For Carlo, the crossing instilled in him a new sense of reality and erased his conviction of cowardice. Each man, then, through dependence on the other, fulfills himself as never before. Each has experienced the end of his loneliness and isolation. It is also of note that, in addition to the importance of the final scene as regards its play action and thematic implications, the crossing is the most difficult, if not crucial, portion to present on stage. Besides the extreme physical strength and endurance Blondín would need if he actually bore Carlo on his back, this scene places heavy technical burdens on the director. Alegría anticipated such demands, however, and in addition to an elevated walkway for Carlo and the proper costumes to effect his being carried, he advises the use of black light to help create the suspense of the moment and to accentuate the dramatic movements which, for this viewer, approximate those of a ballet.

For anyone acquainted with these two dramas, it may indeed seem unlikely that they are by the same author. *Remigio el huaquero* is of traditional fare with no dramatic or technical innovations. With the exception of a convincing portrayal of a huaquero, a little known character outside of the Andean society, the play offers a minimum of evidence to substantiate Alegría's capability and originality as a dramatist. *El cruce*, on the other hand, strongly evinces his capabilities in this regard and further establishes his reputation as a creative artist. It is equally significant that Alegría's second play typifies the goals of the latest generation of dramatists in Peru: it is directed at a universal audience and, with a general absence of any regionalistic appeal, is a rejection of the popular dramatic formulas of the past. Carlo and Blondín, for instance, do not represent any national racial or social type, and their language does not reflect any attempt to "Peruvianize" the play. Their dialogue, in fact, suggests that one of Alegría's strong points is his controlled, yet imaginative, use of language. Throughout the drama, for example, the author is careful to maintain the separate identities of the two characters, and, to this end, their dialogue is a spontaneous exchange free of any unnatural or extraneous digressions or lapses. At the same time, nonetheless, the dialogue gradually and subtly conditions the viewer to accept the momentary appearance of the third dramatic being, Icarón. In dramatic as well as thematic terms, therefore, Icarón represents more than the physical and mental coordination of Carlo and Blondín's beings. For the characters and the viewer, Icarón is a third, although imagined, character. It is important to reiterate that Icarón is not a sudden or unexpected creation. As early as the third scene, Carlo describes what he is to be:

> *Yo* no voy a cruzar con *usted.* No no. Mire. De lo que se trata aquí es de crear un tercer equilibrista. Ni usted ni yo cruzamos, no los dos juntos tampoco, sino otro. . . . Un tercer equilibrista, ése va a cruzar el Niágara. (*El cruce*, p. 28)

It is during the crossing, however, that Alegría's artistic command of the language is most admirably executed. Throughout the scene, Blondín and Carlo alternately speak very loudly (the italicized portions), as if they were speaking over the sound of the falls, and in more softened apartes, to indicate their separate thoughts and reactions to the feat. The effect of this technique is an intriguing combination of their own dialogue and their interior monologue.

> BLONDIN: *Y ahora, ¿no quieres ser equilibrista?*
> CARLO: *No. Yo soy científico.*
> BLONDIN: Se te nota. Pasa en un pie, un pie en el alambre y otro en el aire. . .
> CARLO: Usted podría volar.
> BLONDIN: . . . sobre el río, en zig-zag, por donde quiera, porque el espacio está cruzado de mil alambres invisibles e infinitos, y yo puedo caminarlos todos. (*El cruce*, p. 50)

As the scene progresses, however, it also becomes clear that, in his apartes, each character is repeating significant phrases uttered by the other during the preceding segments of the play.

> BLONDIN: Será un paseo lindísimo, Blondín, yo iré muy atento, de pura novelería, porque ¿miedo?

CARLO: Nada más que aire por todos lados.
BLONDIN: Usted es el mejor equilibrista del mundo. Usted nunca caerá al vacío.
CARLO: Nada más que aire brillante y el sol, me parece que puedo caminar fuera del alambre. (*El cruce*, p. 51)

This reversal of dialogue and its expression in the form of interior monologue is Alegría's most effective use of language in *El cruce* because, besides indicating the extent to which each has accepted the other's thoughts and emotional reaction to their feat, it reinforces their perfect state of psychological coordination (the concept of Icarón) and their mutual acceptance of the challenge.

El cruce also differs from *Remigio el huaquero* with regard to the basic structural changes Alegría has made. Namely, he has turned to the use of brief and dramatically simple scenes in place of longer and more elaborate acts. With this change, he has made excellent use of offstage voices and music and such technical aids as lighting, sound effects, and costuming. His attention to the technical aspects of his work is particularly notable in the transition between scenes. At the end of the fifth scene, for instance, after the final decision has been made to cross the falls, Blondín puts his arm over Carlo's shoulder and they exit to the rising thunder of the falls. Since this sound does not cease until the final curtain, it assures that the anxiety of the fifth scene is sustained and transmitted to the last, which begins with Carlo and Blondín on the tightrope. To be sure, the impressive structural unity and dramatic intensity of *El cruce* is largely due to Alegría's preoccupation with every aspect of his creation, especially the technical.

There can be no doubt that *El cruce sobre el Niágara* is among the most significant Peruvian dramas of the past decade, if not the past thirty years. In addition to its national recognition, it is also one of the few dramas by a contemporary Peruvian to be received favorably by the international audience. Partial explanation of its success lies in the universality of the characters and in the confident thematic conclusion that the anguish of the human condition can be relieved. From the first to the last scene, *El cruce* is an optimistic expression of faith in man's struggle to give life meaning. For this reason, the play is not a pessimistic evaluation of man and his ability to escape the solitude of his existential vacuum. Moreover, Carlo and Blondín reach their personal fulfillment through absolute trust and dependence on each other, and their victory constitutes Alegría's contention that man cannot, and is not meant to wage, his existential struggle alone.

To conclude, it should be noted that Alegría is in the process of completing a third drama, *El terno blanco*. It is expected to be a long play divided into three acts with nine scenes and nine interludes. This work has been in progress for several years and likely is still incomplete due to the numerous demands on Alegría as a professional artist and administrator. Its delayed appearance reinforces our belief that Alegría's production is still in a formative stage and promises to be as multifaceted as his career interests. But it is the balance of these interests, however contradictory they may seem, which best explains his success and points to a meaningful future for him as an activist in the Peruvian theatre.

During the recent years, an era in which increasing numbers of women have sought improved social and professional opportunities, the role and achievements of female dramatists throughout Latin America have been more favorably acknowledged, but not without the frequent barbs of the severest critics. There can be little doubt that many women have been reticent to publicize their creative endeavors for fear of negative evaluation and consequences wrought by a society which is still more receptive to the production of their male counterparts. From a factual point of view, for instance, since the 1940's in Peru there have been only eleven women dramatists known to write thirty-one plays whereas approximately seventy male dramatists have written more than one hundred and seventy works for the stage.[59] To illustrate more clearly the diminished role of the female in the past decade of the Peruvian theatre, one only needs to point out that since 1965 no more than three women have seen their works presented: Sarina Helfgott, Sara Joffré, and Elena Portocarrero. Moreover, Helfgott and Portocarrero have not written any plays since 1966, the year in which they released *Hoy no, mañana tampoco* and *La Señorita Canario*, respectively. Only Joffré has persevered.

Sara Joffré was born in 1935 in Callao, the port city of Lima, and since her early teen years has nurtured a keen interest in the theatre. In her late adolescence, for example, she founded a theatre group for children under the auspices of the Biblioteca del Callao and for several years served as its principal playwright and director. By her mid-twenties, her activities as a writer and director had already elevated her to a respected level of competence among her peers. Joffré has modestly commented on the early years of her professional preparation and recognition in this way:

> En 1960 por una extraña casualidad estuve de delegado en Cuba para una reunión internacional de jóvenes de América Latina y fue una experiencia muy importante donde, creo, aprendí mucho. En 1962 escribí y pusieron en escena [*Cuento alrededor de un circulo de espuma*]. Eso me sirvió para obtener una bolsa de viaje del Consejo Británico y otra del Centro Peruano de Teatro con lo que me las ingenié para estar un año en Europa, dos meses en Inglaterra y el resto en muchos sitios.[60]

Upon her return to Lima in 1963, Joffré was quick to revive her participation in the theatre by founding Homero, teatro de grillos, a children's theatrical group for which she has composed and directed approximately fifty works. Now, more than a decade later, this group is practically an institution in Lima and has an enormous repertoire for the regularly scheduled delight of the youth of the Capital city. Joffré's persistent concern for Homero has clearly hindered her developing her interests in what may be termed here adult drama. But she has done so without apparent regret, as attested by her own judgment that "el asunto [Homero] todavía va muy bien. Giras—muchas puestas etc" (Joffré, letter to Morris). Her laudatory efforts to instill in youth the worth of the

59. Robert J. Morris, "The Peruvian Theatre, 1946-1966," Ph.D. dissertation, University of Kentucky, 1968.

60. Sara Joffré, Lima, Peru, to Robert J. Morris, Lubbock, Texas, 24 May 1974, *in* Texas Tech University Library, Lubbock. Subsequent reference to this correspondence will be indicated parenthetically by Joffré, letter to Morris.

theatre (demonstrated in her leadership and contributions to the so-called Teatro infantil) are too often overlooked as an invaluable service to the future generations of writers who can only profit from a public already appreciative of the genre as an artistic expression. Nor is the foregoing to imply that Joffré is included herein as a token recognition of the female artist in Peru. On the contrary, for more than ten years she has been a key figure in what she terms Teatro para adultos, and, in addition to the aforementioned *Cuento alrededor de un círculo de espuma*, she has written *En el jardín de Mónica* (1962), *Historia de los tocadores de tambor* (1966), *Embargo* (1967), *Pre-texto* (1969), and *El embudo de la ley* (1970). Other works include *Versión de Fuenteovejuna del Galpón: Monólogo de Laurencia*, an adaptation of this famous moment of the Golden Age drama by Lope de Vega; and *Tríptico del Boom*, a theatrical portrayal of monologues by three of the masters of the contemporary Hispanic-American novel: Julio Cortázar, Mario Vargas Llosa, and Gabriel García Márquez. The two latter works remain unpublished, however, and are not included in this study.

Joffré's first two dramas, *Cuento alrededor de un círculo de espuma* and *En el jardín de Mónica*, were composed and presented in the same program by Grupo Alba in El Club de Teatro in Lima in 1962. This performance, however, was typical of the debut of many writers in that it was not a reliable indicator of Joffré's artistic or dramatic capabilities. Moreover, as one reviews its impact upon the Peruvian theatre of the early 1960's, Joffré's initial presentations appear relatively unimportant, particularly in view of the fact that they could not compete with the commercial and lingering costumbrista theatre of the time. As such, Joffré's debut received little attention, and, even now, these two works seem to have passed into oblivion. From an historical standpoint, nonetheless, they merit recognition as the first evidence of what is termed, at least in this study, the third generation of postwar dramatists in Peru. They were staged three years before any of the works by Julio Ortega or Alonso Alegría, for instance, and contain all of the principal elements that subsequently have come to characterize the most recent theatre in Peru: they are brief, of universal appeal and poetic design, and simply elaborated with regard to the use of language and play action.

Within the scope of Joffré's total production, *Cuento alrededor de un círculo de espuma*,[61] her first composition, should be remembered for introducing this author's predominating theme, the contrasting worlds of reality and fantasy. Specifically, all of Joffré's plays since 1962, with the possible exception of *Pre-texto*, dramatize her contention that those who can exist within the world of fantasy, safe from the anguish of reality, are to be envied. The work concerns Trigo and Lechuguita, circus clowns who have worked together for years with the conviction that their mission is to distort reality for the sole purpose of turning tragedy into comedy. Elena, a lonely young woman, visits the clowns in the second scene and confesses that she believes them to be sad, that their com-

61. Sara Joffré, *Cuento alrededor de un círculo de espuma. En el jardín de Mónica* (Lima: Exprinter, 1962), 6-35.

edy is actually inspired by the tragedy of their real lives. Their reply, which is at first as absurd as it is poetic, is that they have intentionally surrounded themselves with a symbolic circle of foam to distort all they see. The clowns explain that they live in a world of fantasy in order to protect themselves from the world beyond, the world of needless suffering. In addition, those who look on them are unable to discern the reality of the clowns' existence because of the foam and because what is ordinarily tragic they turn to fantastic comedy. The third scene takes place sometime later, after Elena has become frustrated because she is unable to appreciate the reason for the circle of foam and the clowns' fantastic existence. She longs for their companionship, but leaves the circus because she is left outside the circle. In the final scene, Elena returns having realized that the only way to transcend the reality of her frustration and solitude is to be with the clowns in the circle. The play ends as she symbolically enters the circle and converts her personal tragedy to comedy.

Cuento alrededor de un círculo de espuma, as already stated, stood in stark contrast with the majority of plays being presented in Lima in the early 1960's. But it was her desire for nonconformity that launched Joffré as a serious artist and invested this and her other creations with real purpose—to introduce and experiment with various philosophical and artistic aspects of the avant-garde drama. Chronologically, then, Joffré's was a bold novelty in Peru, coming only twelve years after the debut of Ionesco's *La Cantatrice Chauve*, the play most often credited with introducing the recent tradition of the avant-garde theatre. This is not to imply that Joffré's play is an imitation of any dramatic technique or trend in particular, but neither is it to deny that the literary purist may detect some indebtedness to such "isms" as the surreal or absurd. The more important consideration is that this work formally introduced Joffré and the third generation of writers and the common denominator of all their works: the renovation of the national drama. And from this perspective, it would seem premature, if not restrictive, to attempt any strict categorization of the work of Joffré or of any other member of Peru's third generation of dramatists inasmuch as this spirit of change is still their common bond.

As one turns to Joffré's first work with a critical intent, few weaknesses are evident. The most disturbing of these occur in the second and third scenes when the clarity of the play action is overshadowed by rather obscure plays on words and metaphorical allusions. These complications unfortunately spawn confusion and jeopardize the already complex dramatization of the thematic interests that are couched in the contrasts between the clowns' fantasies and Elena's frustrated attempt to cope with reality. Fortunately, however, none of these lapses is long enough to impair the dramatic credibility of the characters. Moreover, it should be noted that Joffré exhibits considerable skill in maintaining the essential balance between the characters' human and puppetlike qualities and only in the final scene does she draw them as marionettes. This change is subtly effected and impressively enhances that final poetic moment in which the past absurdities of Elena's past human condition are highlighted and then rejected by her fantastic escape.

En el jardín de Mónica,[62] a one-act play in three brief scenes, is like her first in that it suggests that man can turn his anguished existence into a joyous one by erecting a protective wall of fantasy. And even though the escape from reality may be only temporary, this play suggests that the escape is worth the effort. *En el jardín de Mónica* is a portrayal of one little girl's belief in a world of fantasy and of the way in which her wonderland, a garden, becomes a refuge for two other children who are products of the reality beyond the garden wall. Mónica, who has created a world of her own within the walls of a rundown and littered garden, is unaware of her impoverished surroundings because, through her imagination and fantasy, everything there is dear and beautiful to her. In the second scene her fantasy is threatened by the arrival of a young girl who, coming from beyond the wall, is naturally suspicious of Mónica's tales such as those of the invisible bird that sings and of the flowers that grow in the garden. All the girl can see is a pile of decomposed bones and feathers and some rubbish piled up in the corner. The visitor is nevertheless fascinated by Mónica's charm and, by rejecting her own skeptic and realistic outlook, is also able to enter into the wonderland of fantasy. Mónica tells her that a prince is soon to arrive for a party with them, and, at that moment, a young boy climbs the garden wall in search of his kite and joins the girls. When Mónica is gone, the girl is thus left with the boy, her prince. Before her own departure, the girl tells him of Mónica's wonderland and, just as she was captivated by her own imagination, so is the boy. But as he sits alone, anxiously waiting for Mónica to return and show him her treasures, a man enters, takes him by the arm, and leads him away.

En el jardín de Mónica, like Joffré's first drama, is ostensibly dependent on a childish simplicity in its dramatic artistry and thematic execution. But there can be no doubt that if Joffré had failed to perpetuate the infantile tone and their imagined milieu, the contrast between the characters' world of fantasy and reality would have been blurred and, in turn, the thematic impact weakened, if not sacrificed. In order to maintain this simplicity, the author resorts to linguistic patterns typical of very young people and to dialogues which are realistic reproductions of the simple, emotional, and responsive language one would expect to hear from any child in Monica's garden. There are no long passages, the topic of conversation is continuously changed, and every word is aimed at underlining the naturally inquisitive and imaginative nature of the youngsters. Among these, Mónica is the principal character because everything depends on the way she predominates the play action, even in her absence. The girl and the boy are well delineated as typical children who, until they are in the garden, have never been allowed to forget the demands which their materialistic world has forced upon them So when their spell is broken and they are forced to leave the garden, one cannot help but sympathize with their plight. And, of course, this is the response that Joffré seeks in the mature audience because it brings one to realize the extent to which man is enslaved by his own struggle to exist in the real world.

62. *Ibid.,* 37-80.

The work is sound structurally, with the first and final scenes being the most admirably executed. In the initial scene, the principal focus is on Mónica's fantasy and the garden as she (and ultimately her guests) sees it. In the final scene, this veil of fantasy is suddenly drawn away when the man enters. With his appearance, the boy and the audience are suddenly returned to the real world and the shock of the fantastic-realistic contrast is left for everyone who, as the girl and the boy, was overcome by Monica's fantastic wonderland.

Historia de los tocadores de tambor,[63] Joffré's third composition, was completed in 1966 and presented in Lima by the Teatro de la Universidad Católica that same year. Of the five dramas she has written for the general public, it is the most elaborate testimony of her thematic dependence on man's continuous struggle to escape reality by way of his fantasies. In this play the simplistic execution of past dramas gives way to a more complex interplay of dramatic action, dialogues, and philosophical involvement. Regardless of the various technical and even poetic intricacies of *Historia*, its thematic contention is aptly dramatized. The action begins when an elderly drummer joins the dozen or so other people in a small plaza. One of these people, an old lady, offers the drummer some wares from her basket in order to initiate a conversation. This innocent action, however, triggers the imagination of all the bystanders who at once, and for no apparent reason, convince one another that the old man is a marvelous performer who will play only for money. Moreover, he is given no opportunity to put an end to their fantasies because the people now refuse to accept or recognize the reality of the situation. Instead, they insist on paying in the belief that, in exchange, the drummer's music will alleviate the burden of their anguished existence. Three of the four boys present even leave to steal their payment, and an old lady is convinced by her son to pay their last cent to the drummer. Despite his objections, the old man is finally coerced to perform; but his efforts are disastrous and he is suddenly the victim of his public's fantasies when they demand his prosecution for fraud. Thus the fantasy is ended, and the consequences of reality now loom over the drummer who, when brought to trial, can only insist on his innocence as the different characters heap charges against him. The absurdity of the situation is keenly emphasized when the three boys charge the drummer with the responsibility of their theft. The old man's single defender, chosen by random process from among his accusers, finally wins a reprieve when he points out that their charges and lies are no more than a result of their own illusionment. The drummer's saviour, however, is ultimately the fourth youngster who, instead of stealing with his companions, retreated into his own imagination and has now returned as King with an invitation to his party. It is not unexpected, therefore, that the work does not end when the public has realized their illusionment or when confronted by the King. True to the cyclical nature of the theatre of evasion, their return to reality is only momentary as they are quick to accept the King as their saviour and turn with him from the real world to the fantastic.

63. Sara Joffré, *Historia de los tocadores de tambor*, mimeographed (Lima: Teatro de la Universidad Católica, 1966).

Historia de los tocadores de tambor is clearly one of the most significant dramas presented in Peru during the past decade. Unfortunately, it, as so many recent compositions, has yet to receive due consideration from the various quarters of the national theatre even though it illustrates the dramatic excellence and the goals of contemporary artists in Peru and elsewhere in Hispanic America. This work substantially reinforces the efforts by Joffré, among others to facilitate and improve the opportunities for the more recent, yet largely unknown, dramatic expression to be tested in Lima. And there is no doubt that in *Historia*, Joffré is successful in promoting her own interpretation of the theatre of evasion. Finally, *Historia de los tocadores de tambor* incorporates at least one element which, although not of her own invention, was an innovative and compatible addition to Joffré's own production: the use of allegory to reinforce her representative vision and dramatization of modern man's dilemma. With the exception of Salazar Bondy, Joffré is the only dramatist in recent Peru to incorporate this logical complement of the poetic theatre. And there can be no denial that the thematic substance of this play, namely man's contention to alleviate reality by escape into fantasy, is forcefully dramatized by the allegorical designation of the characters. The allegorical innocence of the drummer, for instance, is maintained by the usual sign of the white heart (*corazón blanco*) visible on his chest. A second example is the symbolic role of the two lovers whose sign, which reads "Nosotros sólo tenemos amor, esperamos el vuestro," dictates their decision to pay the drummer with love and to abandon the scene when he is accused. As to be expected in such a piece, love wields no influence and cannot contend with the villainous attitude of the rest of the public.

Embargo (1967),[64] which was originally titled *Una obligación*, has been one of Joffré's most significant plays. This is not because it is her best play, but because it marks the beginning of this author's consciencious efforts to renovate the appeal of her own drama and to experiment even further with her own dramatic aesthetic. It concerns a lonely, but imaginative, young boy and a governmental bill collector who has come to seize the few remaining valuables belonging to the boy's mother, a widow. She is in arrears to the city garbage collectors and is forced to leave her child while she works. The boy is unaware of the impending tragedy and is also unable to perceive the man's sympathetic understanding. As they await the movers, the man is captivated by the youth's marvelous imagination and willingly imitates him in the innocent pleasures he has long since been forced to abandon. But the opportunity to lose his burdens and revel in fantasy are shortlived because the movers soon come and bring with them the harsh demands of the world beyond. *Embargo* thus ends as Joffré's previous plays, with the pathetic reminder of man's enduring condition. In this regard, the play offers nothing new to those already acquainted with Joffré's interpretation of man's evasionist tendency. *Embargo* has, nonetheless, proved of interest to those aficionados in Peru who have generally avoided the

64. Sara Joffré, *Embargo*, mimeographed (Lima: Teatro de la Universidad Católica, 1967).

ostensibly poetic theatre and have maintained a marked preference for works with at least a semblance of reality. If Joffré purposely composed this play with this audience in mind, it must be judged a success. The characterizations, the language, and even the physical setting are realistic. The boy is no more than a typical example of the forlorn child who, when forced to remain in an enclosed, miserable environment, is obliged to resort to his own imagination for amusement. His pitiful innocence immediately attracts the sympathetic response of the man, who, in turn, is no more than the representative victim of society's demands. The dialogue is extraordinarily natural and, although it is intentionally as stereotyped as the characters and their situation, substantially reinforces their ordinary nature. Of special interest is Joffré's ability to capture the infantile quality of the youth and to create the several empathic moods of the man. Their dialogue seems so commonplace and spontaneous that its underlying significance is at first coincidental.

Embargo, then, marks Joffré's turn from the poetic mode of her first works toward an expression that is essentially realistic. And this change, which is particularly apparent in the form and substance of the dialogue of *Embargo*, is accompanied by at least two other basic variations in her dramaturgy in her last two works: the admission of new themes and an increased dependence on character and dramatic situation with which broader portions of the populace can identify. Each of Joffré's last three plays, and particularly *El embudo de la ley*, substantiate her effort to appeal to the vast majority of the Peruvian public that has failed to accept readily any theatre of poetic and intellectual design.

It was not extraordinary, therefore, that Joffré's next play, *Pre-texto* (1969),[65] also reflects her spirit of change, yet conforms to the general directives that had proven successful for several of her contemporaries of the third generation. In fact, *Pre-texto* is strongly reminiscent of Ortega's production with regard to the use of language, the characterizations, and the nature of the dramatic situation. Regardless of the possibility that this play is an imitation of Ortega's work in the technical sense, it is a signal addition to Joffré's own production because it is the first departure from her usual thematic interests and, in general, from her previous dramatic aesthetics. To this end, the play concerns three anonymous personages (1, 2, and 3) who are caught up in a banal, seemingly inane dialogue in which each attempts to force his egotistical views on the others. When words alone do not suffice, 1 and 3 use weapons, a knife and a pistol, to guarantee that the others listen to their respective patter. In the end, when they are about to split up in order to meet other obligations, 1 and 3 give their weapons to 2 so he can dispose of them. But 2 seizes the opportunity and thereupon forces his convictions upon the now defenseless 1 and 3.

Pre-texto thus has few surprises for the experienced aficionado and particularly for those already familiar with the drama of Ortega. For them it would be difficult to deny the latter's influence on Joffré in this play. In *Pre-texto*, as well as in most plays by Ortega, for example, the characters are anonymous stereo-

65. Sara Joffré, *Pre-texto*, typescript, 1974, Texas Tech University Library, Lubbock. Subsequent reference to this play will be indicated parenthetically by *Pre-texto* and appropriate page number.

types, their dialogue is at once universal and ordinary as it points to man's failure to communicate effectively, and any reaction or any recourse to force is shown to be absurd. And it is certain that, in addition to certain technical and artistic similarities, *Pre-texto* and most of Ortega's plays suggest a kinship with the absurd theatre as it is understood to be a comment on man's condition. Both dramatists, for instance, portray man's inability to cope adequately with reality and his ineffectiveness when dealing with even the ordinary problems of his existence. Indeed, the production of both artists, including all of Joffré's other plays, reiterates their ironic proposal that life is an absurd experience that must go on, and that any reaction to one's existence is as absurd as it is futile. Without considering the possibility of Ortega's influence, nonetheless, it would be an exaggeration to maintain that *Pre-texto* is among the best of Joffré's compositions. There is little extraordinary appeal in the characterizations, the dramatic situation, or the philosophic absurdity inherent to the play.

It would be an injustice, however, to fail to mention that Joffré's linguistic prowess, her ability to manipulate the dialogue, is outstanding in this play. In this respect, at least, her work is equal and at times superior to that of Ortega. Of special note are the spontaneity and rapidity with which the dialogue evolves, particularly in the first moments in which the characters begin their discussion by exerting their individual egotistical designs while implying their rejection and alienation of the others' statements. Recognizing that it is difficult, and possibly misleading, to illustrate this author's mastery with only a brief quote, the following lines, taken from the first moments of the play, hopefully give a hint of the general tone and the progression of the dialogue:

1: Entonces vamos a discutir, discutamos.
3: Sí, sí discutamos.
2: ¡Hum!
1: Basta, ¡basta ya de tanto hum! ¿Qué significa tanto hum?
2: ¡Hum! ¡Hum, significa hum!
1: Sí pero no íbamos a decir ¡hum! sino a discutir sobre adónde vamos.
3: Sobre adónde vamos, pero tú deberías decir: vamos a discutir sobre adónde van.
1: ¿No quedó bien claro hace un momento que íbamos a discutir sobre adónde vamos, no sobre adónde van?
3: Ahora ya no me acuerdo. Pero que quede bien claro en todo caso "adónde vamos" se refiere a nosotros. No a ti, ¿esta claro?
1: Entonces, ¿qué es lo que discutiremos? (*Pre-texto*, p. 2)

Regardless of the vitality and originality with prevail in the dialogue of *Pre-texto*, there is the abiding impression that Joffré has not presented the work formally in order to escape the certain accusation that it is her attempt to take advantage of Ortega's proven technique and popularity. And, undeniably, it would be difficult to convince anyone to the contrary. The fate of *Pre-texto*, however, has not deterred nor dissuaded Joffré in her efforts to persevere, to pursue other avenues which lay within her capabilities. In 1967, she also wrote *El embudo de la ley*,[66] which, as previously stated, is her most obvious effort to

66. Sara Joffré, *El embudo de la ley*, mimeographed (Lima: Teatro de la Universidad de San Marcos, 1969).

forfeit the poetic and intellectual intent of past plays in order to reckon directly with man and society. As such, this play is a clear concession to the lingering traditions of realism and regionalism on the Peruvian stage. Its language, the setting, the situation, and even the characters are of recognizably national extraction. Moreover, the intellectual determination of Joffré's past thematic intent is conspicuously absent. In its place, she offers a keen and panoramic criticism of the kind of social and personal injustices which she sees affecting the Peruvian masses.

This brief one-act piece centers on a lowly court clerk who is left to receive complaints and initiate legal proceedings in the absence of the judge. The former is a corrupt individual, however, who takes illegal advantage of his official station for his own gain. His odious deceit is first perpetrated against an Indian (chola) who has come to file against Edilberto, the pernicious seducer of her now pregnant daughter. The chola's plight quickly deteriorates as a result of the numerous delays and illegal costs cast upon her by the man. He, in turn, is in lascivious pursuit of the woman, also a chola, and his lust turns to rage when he discovers that Edilberto is also his competitor for the sexual favors of the woman. It is not surprising, then, when he decides to prosecute Edilberto to the fullest extent of the law and to solicit the first chola's testimony in order to assure his conviction. The clerk's selfish design is brought to an abrupt end, however, when he learns that Edilberto has been murdered for the seduction of a third woman. The clerk's malicious hypocrisy is the lasting impression as he expresses his regrets to Edilberto's uncle, a friend.

El embudo de la ley is thus a brief play with a complicated and fast-paced progression. It is typical of such works in that its brevity facilitates its spontaneity and dramatic intensity. And as intimated before, this work constitutes a broadside attack on a multitude of social ills and human sins. Within the scope of the Peruvian experience, in particular, Joffré points an accusing finger at racial prejudice as she pits the Indian against the mestizo and even the latter against himself. In addition, she is not reluctant to confront numerous other social and human faults such as false pride, economic fraud, hypocrisy, and unacceptable moral standards. Of course, these are universally acknowledged and have been the target of hundreds of dramatists before. But there is no denying that *El embudo de la ley* is Joffré's reflection on these ills as she has observed them in Peru. To this end, the characters are stereotyped representatives of the lower class Indian (cholo) and of the mestizo (criollo), the middle class in Peru, and their language is typically local with regard to the substandard, socially disdained terminology. So without wishing to belabor this work's regionalistic appeal and social criticism, one may conclude that *El embudo de la ley* embodies more than the usual social satire so prevalent during the preceding years. The death of Edilberto points clearly to the tragic consequences of self-indulgence by society as a whole or by any of its supposedly responsible members. For anyone who insists that Joffré's last drama is a concession to popular demands and that its author has transgressed her professional aesthetic, it must be asserted that this play is perhaps her most powerful condemnation of man's absurdity. It is no irony that it won the 1969 Concurso de obras en un Acto, the annual award offered by the prestigious Teatro de la Universidad de San Marcos.

For anyone attempting even a precursory evaluation of Joffré's drama, of initial concern are the basic differences between her first three works, which are easily grouped together due to their thematic and artistic similarity, and her last three plays, each of which is a unique addition to her total production. This discernible variety and Joffré's continued renovative spirit provide easy access to those who desire a critical overview of her adult theatre. But it is also true that, in addition to these visible changes and contrasts, Joffré's theatre contains a number of features that consistently enhance and reinforce the artistic and stylistic unity of her six works. Foremost among these is her persistent portrayal of characters as participants in what may be termed the game of life. Their purpose, the goal of the game, is to escape reality. But true to the tenets of her own theatre of evasion, and also to the theatre of the absurd in general, no one ever wins. Even the apparent victors have deceived themselves inasmuch as their imagined escape is temporary or as fictitious as their role in the game. In Joffré's final play, *El embudo de la ley*, for instance, the man is ultimately deceived by his own hypocrisy and he is unable to discern his true self. He, like all of Joffré's characters, shuns his real being as he pursues an endless search for a fantastic, unattainable identity. Most often this search is motivated by a character's innate, yet representative, desire for self-gain and the possibility of improving his human condition. But, of course, their deceit is heightened even more when they realize that the spoils of victory are as illusive as their ability to play the game of life.

The most perceptive constant, indeed the key to Joffré's dramatic artistry and style, is simplicity. Each of her dramatic situations is in keeping with the general dictates of the brief, usually one-act drama in that they are not complicated and intentionally lack the intricacies of the traditional plot structure. As an essentially poetic dramatist, Joffré prefers those works which can best be described as evocative moments or situations. *El embudo de la ley* again serves as a valid example because, despite the fact that it is ostensibly inspired in the realistic theatre of earlier years, it is a symbolic expression and not devoid of a genuine sense of transcendental universality.

All of the characters in Joffré's drama are also of a simple, clearly distinguishable design and are either symbolic or stereotyped creations of limited dramatic purpose or appeal. Joffré intentionally does not invest them with any profound psychological significance because, in keeping with the poetic and evocative nature of her expression, they are not meant to be person-personages, but person-signs: they represent nothing more than particular aspects of the common human experience with which the audience is invited to identify.

Among all of the features which have substantiated the enduring appeal of Joffré's dramaturgy, none has been more tangible than her adept use of language. Yet even in this regard, it is the simplicity of the dialogues that is outstanding and has assured and perpetuated their spontaneity and natural, ordinary, overtones. With few exceptions, and these are found primarily in her first dramas, the dialogue is brief and unencumbered by obscure poetic subtleties or extraneous digressions. Whether the work in question is the allegorically elaborate *Historia de los tocadores de tambor* or the more mundane *El embudo de la ley*, Joffré's linguistic implications, as well as her thematic stance, are unmistakably clear and succinct.

As one reviews the adult drama of Sara Joffré, the question of her present status as a writer is among the first to arise. And although there is no real evidence that she is certain to reappear as an active writer, one should not assert that, because she has not staged a new work since 1970, she has abandoned her role as a contending dramatist. For the pessimist the inconsistencies of her last three plays may signify a basic instability which has resulted in her quiet withdrawal. But for many others Joffré's silence since 1970 is typical in the career of the serious writer who, in search of excellence, prefers quality, not quantity. For the optimist, Joffré may be expected to reappear with new proof of her abilities.

In 1969, a small volume of seven one-act plays, published under the title *Teatro campesino*,[67] appeared in a number of bookstores in Lima. The author, Víctor Zavala Cataño, was at that time generally unknown as a dramatist except to those few who remembered him as the author of *El gallo*, the 1966 winner of the first Concurso para obras de un acto sponsored by the Teatro de la Universidad de San Marcos. Even fewer realized that in 1960 Zavala had also won the Concurso de teatro escolar sponsored by T.U.S.M. Since the publication of *Teatro campesino*, Zavala has come to the forefront within the ranks of those few dramatists in Hispanic America who successfully employ the theatre to emphasize the continued subjugation of the indigenous masses. In Peru, Zavala is undoubtedly the leading exponent of the so-called teatro comprometido, and, as such, his is a theatre of protest predicated on the socioeconomic subjugation and frustrated aspirations of the Andean Indian. Zavala's theatre, however, is not a revolutionary protest; it is best described as a defense of the principles of evolutionary socialism. Even so, Zavala's political posture is not original or a novelty in the national theatre. Throughout the history of the Hispanic-American theatre, as well as the Peruvian, scores of writers have used the theatre to vent their political views, and many of these have paralleled or preceded Zavala's evolutionary philosophy. The appeal of the vast majority of these writers, however, has proved ephemeral because their works were decidedly propagandistic and lacked those artistic and dramatic features which could have assured their enduring appeal. Zavala has wisely avoided this pitfall and has deservedly gained a permanent position in the Peruvian theatre by expressing his socioeconomic philosophy as an artist rather than as a political propagandist. This is not to imply that Zavala's production is a distortion of the real plight of the Andean Indian. In fact, Zavala is one of the few dramatists

67. Víctor Zavala Cataño, *Teatro campesino* (La Cantuta: Ediciones Universidad Nacional de Educación, 1969). Subsequent reference to this volume will be indicated parenthetically by *Teatro campesino* and appropriate page numbers.

whose works have proven successful in the provincial environment before their premiere in the cosmopolitan centers The lure of his favorable reception in the larger cities has failed to sway Zavala's dedication to the masses, nonetheless, and he has remained in the rural areas to continue his dramatic pursuits. Fortunately, his intentional isolation has not abated his reputation as a dramatist of national prominence.

Despite the inconspicuous nature of his provincial debut, Zavala's beginning was soon recognized as an important indication that the desire for fomenting the national theatre was no longer restricted to Lima and a few other cosmopolitan centers such as Trujillo and Arequipa. But it was just as significant that Zavala's first work was more than a social protest, that it emanates a real concern with nurturing a new appreciation for the dramatic arts among the provincial public. In this regard, it should be noted that Zavala has always been mindful of the aesthetic limitations of his provincial public and for this reason has limited his artistic involvement to those devices and expressions which are readily accepted by the majority of the Indian masses. As a consequence, *La gallina* (*Teatro campesino*, pp. 25-37), as are all his works, is devoid of any obscure symbolic implications or dramatic complexities. It is a brief work in which the campesino is falsely accused and forced to admit that he killed a chicken belonging to the hacienda. His sole accuser is the Cabo, a stereotype of the corrupt official who viciously maligns the Indian to glorify his own position. The cholo's only mistake, however, was to feed the chicken, which he found dead, to his starving family. The consequences of his innocent act are tragically compounded with the news that his son has died from the contaminated meat and that his sick and pregnant wife has been raped by the real culprit, the son of the hacendado. Even the campesino's elderly father fails to offer any consolation or hope. Instead, he tries to sedate his son with coca, to mollify him with his insistence that the Cholo is defenseless against his social master.

La gallina introduces several other constants which also characterize Zavala's dramaturgy: the use of song, pantomime, dance, and a variety of standard poetic devices, such as the sun, moon, and animals, to substantiate the universal and symbolic intent of his drama; dependence on stock characters, such as the hacendado, government officials, and, particularly, the elder cholo who speaks with the voice of experience to his younger counterpart who is more confident that the Indian can improve his lot; and the use of monologue to highlight the thematic conflict and to reflect the Indian's determination.

Among Zavala's remaining pieces, there is one other, *El collar* (*Teatro campesino*, pp. 39-52), which is similar to *La gallina* with regard to the basic theme, story, and dramatic artistry. In addition, *La gallina* and *El collar* focus indirectly on one of Zavala's principal social concerns: the harsh consequences produced when Indian family groups and comunidades are dissolved by those latifundios which will not tolerate their cooperative labor. To this end, *El collar* poignantly dramatizes the struggle of the female who, forced to abandon the protective confines of the community in order to survive, migrates to the city where she is victimized again by the insensitive and corrupt elements of the so-called civilized society. Specifically, the chola, a young maid for an upper-class family, is falsely accused and jailed for stealing a necklace belonging to the Lady. Even the maid's only friend, an elderly chola, is unable to console her; like the old Indian in *La gallina*, she believes the Indian is hopelessly bound by an unjust society and that a rebellious attitude is self-condemning. The play ends when the Lady, who is reminiscent of the Cabo in *La gallina*, maliciously defames her maid only to be reminded that she had lent the necklace to a friend.

Despite the fact that *La gallina* and *El collar* are representative of Zavala's basic thematic and artistic concerns, they are also unique among his production in at least two important ways: they are the only works in which he fails to emphasize the agressive and intellectual aspects of the Indian character, and they are the only ones which do not offer a practical solution to the real problem of the social subjugation of the indigenous masses. In the first instance it is of note that in his other plays the Indian is no longer the stereotyped representative of the intellectually underdeveloped, often dehumanized, and listless peon. Instead, he is an emotionally sensitive, clever, even shrewd character dependent on an innate intelligence rather than on any formal or socially sanctioned instruction. In the second instance, it is to be observed that all of Zavala's plays written after *La gallina* express directly the author's contention that the indigenous masses should organize into comunidades to escape their virtual enslavement. In Zavala's view, these comunidades are best organized in a peaceful and evolutionary fashion. Moreover, he implicitly states that any sustained revolutionary efforts will be detrimental to the eventual integration of the masses into the mainstream of the national social and economic structures. Recognizing that his plea for communal action could appear idealistic or too impersonal to the Indian, Zavala has seen fit to create dramatic situations with which the Indian can readily indentify, and he has expressed his optimistic philosophy of social unity by dramatizing the real and ordinary problems which the Indian must face. There are three works in which Zavala gives a practical example of the futility of any individual effort when compared to the strength and security inherent in collective cooperation.

The first of these, *El cargador* (*Teatro campesino*, pp. 53-88), begins after the protagonist has arrived in the city where he expects to be free of the social and economic bonds of the latifundio. Almost immediately, however, he is duped by a salesman who preys on the Indian's representative naiveté and is jailed when he cannot pay his exaggerated debt. Once freed to work off his debt, the destitute cholo is fortunately accepted and even cared for by a small community of Indian bearers who have banded together for their mutual protection. This experience convinces the Indian of the value of the communal system, and he returns to his village to instill its worth in those who, like him before, still suffer the dictatorial organization of the latifundio.

In *La yunta* (*Teatro campesino*, pp. 145-185), the campesino again leaves his rural environment and finds that he is unable to reckon with the unscrupulous elements of the socioeconomic system he does not understand and, also with a hostile nature against which he is even more helpless. After losing his oxen, which he needed to wage his struggle, to an unscrupulous latifundista, the bereft Indian returns home; now anxious to support the comuneros fighting to end their subjugation by the large hacienda.

The last of these works, *El turno* (*Teatro campesino*, pp. 89-114), is Zavala's longest and most involved with respect to the dramatic situation in which he couches his social criticism. It is also the work which best substantiates Zavala's determination to elaborate his basic theme of evolutionary social change as an artistic, not a propagandistic expression. Despite its length and thematic dramatic involvement, however, *El turno* follows Zavala's usual story development with one noticeable exception—the younger campesino intent on leaving the community is deterred when he heeds the advice of the older cholo, now returned after failing to farm alone in an area near a city. As the elder explains, his return to the community was prompted when the water needed to harvest his crop was expropriated by the power company to produce electric power. When in the company of other cholos he demanded his rights, the company expropriated their lands in lieu of the payment for the electricity the Indians had been forced to accept. The play then ends with the elder's advice to remain in the community and to support the increasing demands of the comuneros for justice. He warns that the Indian must organize to guarantee even the basics which are necessary to his existence.

Zavala's repetition of the basic theme, dramatic situation, and character types in his first five works, and particularly in the last three, admittedly may prove disappointing to any but the unsophisticated audience. But to indict Zavala's work by dwelling on its repetitive elements would be an unjust denial of its more positive artistic merits. It is the blend of Zavala's thematic constancy and artistic elements that has enabled his production to appeal to the Indian audience, for which it is primarily intended, as well as to those who, in addition to supporting his social philosophy, also expect the theatrical expression to reflect some degree of aesthetic sophistication. It is therefore important to reiterate that his should not be considered just a regionalistic or typically costumbrista expression, the sole purpose of which is to reflect, in detail, either the types of characters, the language, or even the physical aspects peculiar to the Andean Indian. This is not to deny that Zavala has found his inspiration, indeed his thematic motives, in this region, but to relegate his works to the realm of purely realistic indigenous drama would be to negate their conspicuous artistic and thematic universality.

Chief among Zavala's artistic devices is his use of song, dance, pantomime, and numerous symbolic and allegorical elements that one ordinarily does not associate with the traditional costumbrista drama in Hispanic America. *El turno*, as an example, includes several moments in which the basic philosophy is dramatically relieved and reinforced with song accompanied by musical instruments, choral response, and a symbolic danza guerrera, in pantomime, in which the Indians' determination to confront their oppressors is manifested.

But these poetic interludes are not Zavala's only attempts to perpetuate the overall symbolic intent of his work. In all of his plays, the characters are, on one level, of a realistic and identifiable regional extraction and, on a second level, of a representative and universal design. In addition to his use of stock Indian characters, as the young, naive peasant and the older, experienced, and sometimes calloused counterpart, Zavala also depends on such allegorical characters as the capitalist, governmental bureaucrat, technocrat, biased members of the judiciary, and, particularly, the malicious latifundista. Secondary, but nonetheless essential to the artistic design of Zavala's craft, is his dependence on lighting effects, stage sets, and such natural phenomena as the rising sun and moon to reinforce the poetic overtones of his work.

There are two of Zavala's works, however, in which he departs from his usual admonition against Indian emmigration to emphasize the direct confrontation between the innately agressive and shrewd character of the cholo and the vile cowardice of the corrupt hacendado. In *El arpista* (*Teatro campesino*, pp. 115-144), the hacendado and his friend, respective allegorizations of oppression and perverted intelligence, become inebriated while listening to the music of an elderly Indian harpist. During the course of their conversation, and with the constant accompaniment of the indigenous folk tunes, the hacendado admits that he is wholly insensitive to the plight of the cholo and even defends his oppressive measures as his legal and patriotic duty. By early morning, when the sun is beginning to rise, the supposedly domesticated comuneros take advantage of his drunken stupor and forcefully take control of the hacienda.

While *El arpista* represents Zavala's determination to vary the dramatic and, to some degree, the basic thematic structure of his work, it is also among the best examples of his artistic capabilities. Of particular note is the interpolated symbolic danza toril, in pantomime, in which the younger and elder Indians presage their victory over their oppressor. From the moment of the dance, until the end of the drama, the bull is sustained as the symbol of the courage and force which the Indian must muster in order to be able to defeat the cowardly hacendado. Then, in the final moments, the now apparently insane hacendado shoots his pistol at the imaginary bull, which, as predicted earlier, has trampled his selfish ambitions and freed the suppressed masses.

The last of Zavala's works, *El gallo* (*Teatro campesino*, pp. 11-24), is perhaps his least representative with regard to its thematic and artistic intent. But there is little doubt that this work has been Zavala's best known since its premiere in 1966 at the Teatro de la Universidad de San Marcos. The most plausible explanation of its success is found in the originality of its dramatic situation, its portrayal of the Indian as a sympathetic yet clever individual, and its genuinely humorous outcome. This work also implies a basic condemnation of those who have perpetuated the subjugated state of the Indian masses; but Zavala's principal focus here is on the ordinary aspects of the individuals involved in this confrontation. For this reason none of the characters are truly stereotyped, the poetic overtones of his other works is conspicuously absent, and the language, dramatic situation and dramatic action are the most realistic of his production.

Succinctly, *El gallo* concerns a group of Indians who, frustrated by their forced labor at the early morning call of the rooster, deceive their boss and lure him into the chicken roost before the usual time. Thereupon they arouse the hacendado who, with the hope of catching the chicken thief, peppers his favored employee with shotgun pellets. This work, then, continues Zavala's broadside attack on the social injustices that plague the Andean cholo, but it also defends the Indian as an individual, not just an insignificant peon in the dehumanized society in which he is forced to exist.

Despite the moderate success of Zavala's plays in the provincial environs of Peru and in Lima, his *Teatro campesino* has elicited a minimum of response from drama critics outside the country. But the plight of Zavala's production beyond the national borders is undoubtedly due to the reticence of most reviewers to consider what, on the basis of the title of his work, must seem little more than the traditional teatro comprometido bound by a repetitious social protest and an inane aesthetic purview. This is a myopic rejection of a dramatist who knows to express his protest with more than a modicum of artistic appeal and originality. In fact, one of the more intriguing facets of Zavala's drama is that the Andean Indian is not portrayed as the naive, lackadaisical individual who is either a burden to society or an obstacle to the national well being. Instead, Zavala emphasizes the positive elements of the Indian character to support his contention that by not integrating the cholo, what he views to be the soul of the national raison d'etre, society is rejecting the very essence of its own being. Just as Zavala's call for the evolutionary integration of the Indian has a regional and a transcendental, universal appeal, so does the artistic elaboration of his drama. For this reason, Zavala's is a stylized, indeed poetic expression that, in his effort to overcome scenic or even photographic realism, more nearly approaches the tenets of modern farce and pantomime than those of the naturalistic theatre of the past. Therefore, and without negating the folkloric or regionalistic scope and inspiration of his production, Zavala's recourse to standard poetic devices, symbols, and allegory promotes the appeal of his work to the cosmopolitan audience that can better appreciate his aesthetic aspirations and the universality of his social protest.

Thus, despite his personal isolation from the mecca of the dramatic arts in Peru, Víctor Zavala merits recognition as one of the most resourceful dramatists in contemporary Peru. This is true because, in a manner as imposing as that of any of his peers in the third generation—Ortega, Joffré, Alegría—Zavala has forced the realization that the real purpose of their common goal of renovating the theatre is, first, to return their art form to all sectors of the Peruvian public and, second, to reflect the Peruvian experience to those beyond the national borders.

For those who have kept abreast of the achievements of those writers and theatre groups that have promoted the Peruvian theatre during the past three decades, there can be little doubt that considerable progress has been made toward renovating the aesthetic, thematic, and even the social values which, until the end of the Second World War, bound this theatre to a dismal past and promised little hope for improvement. But it is true also that, despite the individual efforts and achievements of dramatists such as Salazar Bondy, Ríos, and Solari Swayne during the 1950's and 1960's, the most significant and visible changes in the overall thematic, technical, and aesthetic posture of the Peruvian theatre have occurred since 1965 and have been made in a collective fashion by those younger dramatists who may be grouped together as the third generation. Moreover, there is ample cause for optimism with regard to the continuing revival of this theatre because the creative efforts of writers such as Ortega, Alegría, Joffré, and Zavala and of theatre groups such as Teatro de la Universidad Católica, Teatro de la Universidad de San Marcos, and Histrión have not yet terminated. For this reason, in fact, it would seem precipitous at this time to make any final conclusions concerning the enduring value of this generation's total dramaturgy or to anticipate its future status. To do so, in essence, would be to suggest that the renovation of the Peruvian theatre has ended or that it has already achieved full independence from its past tradition and its goal of aesthetic solidarity. And while this is not the case, neither can there be any doubt that, without the progressive momentum of this generation, the national revival of the dramatic arts would have begun to wither in the 1960's and that, by now, the Peruvian theatre would be practically defunct.

As one looks to the future of the drama in Peru, however, there are still serious obstacles that confront every aspect of its survival. Foremost among these is the need to inflate public support of the theatre so that new writers will be encouraged and so that those who are already active may strengthen their own efforts. But it is true also that popular support will never increase substantially until the theatre groups and the dramatists, through their combined efforts, can appeal directly to the general populace with works which incorporate the essential goals of the creative artist with the more mundane preferences of the theatre-going public in Peru. Fortunately, the Peruvian theatre ensemble has not overlooked this problem entirely and there already are those individuals and institutions, such as Alonso Alegría and the Teatro Nacional Popular, the abiding goal of which is to popularize the theatre without forfeiting all of their artistic sensibilities or converting the drama into a propagandistic instrument. Even more significant is the realization that there is also considerable variety among the writers and groups who have been active during the past ten years. For example, whereas Ortega's work may be philosophically unpalatable to the masses, Alegría's first work, Joffré's last, and all of Zavala's production are clearly intended for the less demanding audiences who appreciate the simplistic artistic intentions of these plays and can more easily accept them as a reflection of society in general. This is not to imply that the Peruvian theatre should or is reverting to a regionalistic expression similar to that of its past, but that the present group of dramatists and theatre groups are constantly experimenting with their own dramatic interests and with public reaction in an effort to perpetuate, hopefully for years to come, the spirit of their country's theatre renewal.

BIBLIOGRAPHY

Alegría, Alonso. *El cruce sobre el Niágara.* Mimeographed. Lima: Teatro de la Universidad de San Marcos, 1969.

——. "El teatro es una infección." *Textual, Revista de Artes y Letras*, 2(septiembre 1971):4.

Cajiao Salas, Teresa. "Balance del Año Teatral 1972 en Lima." *Latin American Theatre Review*, 8(Fall 1974):67-73.

Jiménez Borja, José. "Un hallazgo inesperado." *Mar del sur*, 23(septiembre-octubre 1952): 34.

——. *Pachacámac.* Lima: La Rama Florida, 1965.

Joffré, Sara. *Cuento alrededor de un círculo de espuma. En el jardín de Mónica.* Lima: Exprinter, 1962.

——. *Historia de los tocadores de tambor.* Mimeographed. Lima: Teatro de la Universidad Católica, 1966.

——. *Embargo.* Mimeographed. Lima: Teatro de la Universidad Católica, 1967.

——. *El embudo de la ley.* Mimeographed. Lima: Teatro de la Universidad de San Marcos, 1969.

Jones, Willis Knapp. *Behind Spanish American Footlights.* Austin: University of Texas Press, 1966.

Lubbock. Texas Tech University Library. Alonso Alegría. *The Buried Palace.* Typescript.

——. Texas Tech University Library. Sara Joffré, Lima, Peru, to Robert J. Morris, Lubbock, Texas, 24 May 1974.

——. Texas Tech University Library. Sara Joffré. *Pre-texto.* Typescript.

——. Texas Tech University Library. Julio Ortega, Lima, Peru, to Robert J. Morris, Lubbock, Texas, 28 September 1971.

Luchting, Wolfgang A. "Une saison a Lima" *Latin American Theatre Review*, 9(Spring 1976):81-84.

Morris, Robert J. "The Peruvian Theatre, 1946-1966." Ph.D. dissertation. University of Kentucky, 1968.

——. "The Theatre of Sebastián Salazar Bondy." *Latin American Theatre Review*, 4(Fall 1970):59-71.

——. "The Theatre of Julio Ortega." *Latin American Theatre Review*, 6(Fall 1972): 41-51.

——. "Ricardo Palma and the Contemporary Peruvian Theatre." *Romance Notes*, 15(Spring 1973):465-468.

——. "The Theatre of Juan Ríos Rey." *Latin American Theatre Review*, 7(Spring 1974): 81-95.

——. "Alonso Alegría: Dramatist and Theatrical Activist." *Latin American Theatre Review*, 9(Spring 1976):49-55.

Murga, José Hesse, ed. *Teatro peruano contemporáneo.* 2nd ed. Madrid: Aguilar, 1963.

Natella, Arthur A., Jr. "Enrique Solari Swayne and *Collacocha.*" *Latin American Theatre Review*, 4(Spring 1971):39-44.

Núñez, Estuardo. *La literatura peruana en el siglo XX.* Mexico City: Pormaca, 1965.

Ortega Cuentas, Julio. *Teatro.* Lima: Teatro de la Universidad Católica, 1965.

——. *Varios rostros del verano.* Mimeographed. Lima: Teatro de la Universidad Católica, 1968.

——. "Mesa pelada." *Textual, Revista de Artes y Letras*, 2(septiembre 1971):20-29.

Oviedo, José Miguel. "Sebastián Salazar Bondy en su teatro." *Revista Peruana de Cultura*, 7-8(junio 1966):70-97.

Podestá A., Bruno. "Teatro nacional: Un teatro popular o la popularización del teatro?" *Latin American Theatre Review*, 7(Fall 1973):33-41.

———. "Del T.U.C., su evolución y sus montajes." *Latin American Theatre Review*, 6(Fall 1972):87-90.

Portal, Magda. *Flora Tristán, Precursora.* Santiago, Chile: n.p., 1944.

Portocarrero, Elena. *La corcova. Hoy no, mañana tampoco.* Lima: Ediciones Caballo de Troya, 1966.

Quesada, Aurilio Miró, ed. *Teatro peruano contemporáneo.* Lima: Editorial Huascarán, 1948.

Reedy, Daniel R., and Robert J. Morris. "The Lima Theatre, 1966-67." *Latin American Theatre Review*, 1(Fall 1967):26-38.

Ribeyro, Julio Ramón. *Vida y pasión de Santiago el pajarero.* Lima: Universidad Nacional Mayor de San Marcos, 1965.

———. *El último cliente.* Mimeographed. Lima: Teatro de la Universidad de San Marcos, 1966.

Ríos Rey, Juan. *El mar.* Mimeographed. Lima: Compañía Lucía Irurita, 1954.

———. *Teatro.* Lima: n.p., 1961.

Rivera Saavedra, Juan. *1999.* Mimeographed. Lima: Histrión, 1963.

———. *Los Ruperto.* Mimeographed. Lima: Histrión, 1965.

———. *Teatro de humor negro.* Lima: Ediciones Arte Futuro, 1967.

Roca Rey, Bernardo. *Loys.* Pp. 6-32 in *Máscara.* Lima: Dirección de Educación Artística y Extensión Cultural, 1950.

———. *Muerte de Atahualpa.* Mimeographed. Lima: Asociación de Artistas Aficionados, 1957.

Rodil y Gayoso, José Ramón. *La defensa del Callao por don José Ramón Rodil durante el período comprendido entre la capitulación de Ayacucho y el embarque en la* Britón. Madrid: Imprenta Palomeque, 1930.

Salazar Bondy, Sebastián. *Seis juguetes.* Lima: Editorial Nuevos Rumbos, 1958.

———. *Teatro.* Buenos Aires: Editorial Losada, 1961.

———. *La escuela de los chismes.* Mimeographed. Lima: Histrión, 1963.

———. *El fabricante de deudas. Flora Tristán.* Lima: Ediciones Nuevo Mundo, 1964.

———. *El Rabdomante.* Mimeographed. Lima: Casa de la Cultura Peruana, 1965.

———. *Obras*, vol. 1. Lima: n.p., 1967.

Sánchez, Luis Alberto. *Una mujer sola contra el mundo.* Buenos Aires: n.p., 1937.

Seyffert, Oskar. *Dictionary of Classical Antiquities.* Revised and edited by Henry Nettleship and James E. Sandys. New York: Meridian, 1958.

Solari Swayne, Enrique. *Collacocha.* Lima: Populibros peruanos, 1964.

———. *La Mazorca.* Mimeographed. Lima: Casa de la Cultura Peruana, 1966.

———. *Ayax Telamonio.* Mimeographed. Lima: Asociación de Artistas Aficionados, 1969.

Tamayo Vargas, Augusto. *Literatura peruana*, vol. 2. Lima: José Godard, 1965.

Vidal, Hernán. "*Esa luna que empieza* y Maeterlinck: la contemporaneidad modernista." *Latin American Theatre Review*, 6(Spring 1973):5-11.

Zavala Cataño, Víctor. *Teatro campesino.* La Cantuta, Peru: Ediciones Universidad Nacional de Educación, 1969.